The dreamer awakes, the shadow goes by.
The tale I have told you, that tale is a lie.
But listen to me bright maiden, proud youth,
The tale is a lie,
What it tells is the truth.
- Anonymous -

ONE DARK NIGHT

MAD GASSERS, BLACK GHOSTS & AMERICA'S OTHER SINISTER STRANGERS

BY TROY TAYLOR

AN AMERICAN HAUNTINGS INK BOOK

ONE DARK NIGHT

MAD GASSERS, BLACK GHOSTS, AND AMERICA'S OTHER SINISTER STRANGERS

ISBN: 978-1-7352706-2-3

Published by American Hauntings Ink
228 South Mauvaisterre Street - Jacksonville Il - 62650
www.americanhauntingsink.com

Cover Design by April Slaughter
Interior Design by Troy Taylor

Printed in the United States of America

The clock on the nightstand seemed unbearably loud. Aline Kearney glanced over at it again. The luminous hands of the clock read just before 11:00 p.m. She and her sister, Martha, who came to stay with Aline sometimes when Aline's husband, Bert, worked at night, had stayed up far too late.

And they had kept their children up too late. As, with Martha's little boy, Roger, was asleep in her children's bedroom, tucked into the small bed across the room from Aline's daughter, Carol Anne, who had just turned two.

Aline felt movement on the bed beside her, and heard a murmur from her oldest daughter, Dorothy, who was sleeping next to her. Her cousin Roger had taken Dorothy's bed for the night, so Aline had moved her into the master bedroom. Bert wouldn't be home for hours yet.

Aline smiled in the darkness as the thought of her children and husband. She and Bert had been married just four years earlier, and their two daughters had quickly followed. Bert had a good job as a taxi driver, and they had a nice home in one of the better parts of Mattoon.

She didn't see how anything could go wrong. Nothing is perfect, she thought, but my life my life just might be.

Aline tucked a light blanket around Dorothy and turned over to try and close her eyes. She was tired, but waiting with her sister was almost so fun that she found it hard to sleep.

It was a warm night, and the window near the bed was open. Aline sighed a little when she smelled the scent of the flowers that had been planted outside the window. Fall would

SEPTEMBER 1, 1944

MATTOON, ILLINOIS

The clock on the nightstand seemed unbearably loud.

Aline Kearney glanced over at it again. The luminous hands of the clock read just before 11:00 p.m. She and her sister, Martha, who came to stay with Aline sometimes when Aline's husband, Bert, worked at night, had stayed up far too late.

And they had kept their children up too late, as well. Martha's little boy, Roger, was asleep in her children's bedroom, tucked into the small bed across the room from Aline's daughter, Carol Anne, who had just turned two.

Aline felt movement on the bed beside her and heard a murmur from her oldest daughter, Dorothy, who was sleeping next to her. Her cousin Roger had taken Dorothy's bed for the night, so Aline had moved her into the master bedroom. Bert wouldn't be home for hours yet.

Aline smiled in the darkness as she thought of her children and husband. She and Bert had been married just four years earlier, and their two daughters had quickly followed. Bert had a good job as a taxi driver, and they had a nice home in one of the better parts of Mattoon.

She didn't see how anything could go wrong. Nothing is perfect, she thought, but my life just might be.

Aline tucked a light blanket around Dorothy and turned over to try and close her eyes. She was tired, but visiting with her sister was almost so fun that she found it hard to sleep.

It was a warm night, and the window near the bed was open. Aline sighed a little when she smelled the scent of the flowers that had been planted outside the window. Fall would soon be here, but she planned to enjoy every bit of summer they had left.

But was the smell of the flowers getting stronger?

A sickeningly sweet odor filled the bedroom. It was much stronger than flowers. It seemed to flow through the bedroom, causing her to nearly choke. What could it be?

As she lay there, Aline began to feel a peculiar prickling in her legs and lower body. Everything was growing numb! As she turned and tried to get out of bed, she realized that her limbs were paralyzed.

And Aline started to scream.

Her scream awakened Martha, who had been sleeping on the couch in the living room. In moments, she was at Aline's bedroom door, knocking frantically.

"What's wrong?" Martha called. "What's the matter?"

Martha twisted the knob and opened the door. As she stepped inside, she gagged on the sweet stench that filled the room. She ran to the bed and took her sister by the hand, urging her to get up.

"I can't!" Aline told her. "I can't feel my legs! Take Dorothy and get help!"

Martha scooped up the little girl and ran into the living room with her. She was now stirring and confused about what was happening. Then she began to vomit all over the couch.

Martha was now frantic. Something terrible was happening, and they had three small children in the house. She didn't know what to do. Instead of telephoning for help, she ran to the front door, screaming as she went.

Martha's cries - as well as Aline's cries from the bedroom - had awakened the neighbors, including the Robertsons, who lived next door. Mrs. Robertson was the first out the door, and she grabbed hold of the screaming woman and asked her what was wrong. As soon as Martha started to explain, the other woman went back into her home and called the police.

Mr. Robertson, meanwhile, rushed next door to the Kearney house to make sure that everyone was okay. Once Aline assured him that she wasn't hurt, he searched the yard and the surrounding neighborhood for any sign of a prowler but found nothing.

By this time, lights had started to appear in the windows of other nearby homes. Faces could be seen on front porches, but most of the people they belonged to didn't venture too far into the darkness. Most of those faces belonged to neighborhood women - their husbands had gone off to the war - and if there was an intruder on the scene, they didn't want to encounter him.

Because, of course, it was most definitely a man.

A few of the older men on the block came outside in their bathrobes and slippers; flashlights gripped in their fists. They looked around, whispered to each other, and waited for the police to arrive.

Even after a patrol car with two officers inside arrived at the scene, they didn't fare any better than Mr. Robertson had. They walked around the neighborhood and looked at the Kearney yard, but there was no sign of a prowler.

So, what had caused Aline Kearney's strange paralysis? Both she and her sister had smelled some kind of gas or anesthetic in the bedroom. One of the policemen suggested it might have been ether or chloroform but for what purpose? If someone had sprayed gas into the room, was he planning to rob the house? Aline admitted that they did have money in their home. Could that have been what an intruder was looking for? If it was, why go to the trouble of trying to "gas" his victims?

After answering questions from the police, Aline tried to settle herself back into bed. Dorothy had stopped throwing up, but her feeling of weakness and nausea would last until the following morning. Aline had gotten the worst of the gas. Her paralysis soon faded, but she would later complain of burned lips and a parched mouth and throat from exposure to the gas.

By 11.45 p.m., the search by the police officers - and the Kearneys' shaken neighbors - would be called off. The police left the house with instructions to call if anything else strange occurred.

And it would.

Around 12.30 the following morning, Bert Kearney arrived home. He often worked the overnight shift as a cab driver but had received word about the incident at his home and hurried home to make sure his wife and children were safe. The call he had received on the radio wasn't clear about what had happened, though. Something about gas? And his wife is sick? He had no idea what was going on.

As Bert turned into the driveway of his home, his headlights swept over the side of the house, catching a figure standing outside one of the windows. He jammed on the brakes, pulled the hand brake, and flung open the taxi's door. Was that man looking into his and Aline's bedroom window?

Bert called out loudly and started to run toward the figure, who suddenly turned, aware that he had been spotted. As Bert later described him, the man was very tall, dressed in black form-fitting clothing, and wearing a tight, black cap on his head. He stood outside the same window through which Aline reported the gas had been sprayed less than two hours earlier.

The figure ran with Bert in hot pursuit. The prowler's long legs quickly outpaced the stride of Bert Kearney, and he vanished into the darkness. Bert broke off the chase and ran back to his house. Fumbling with his keys, he rushed inside and went directly to the master bedroom.

Aline, Martha, and the three children looked up in surprise. They were all huddled on the bed, their eyes wide with excitement and fright. When Aline saw her husband, she burst into tears. Bert did his best to comfort her, but he also suggested that they all pack some things to leave. They'd spend the rest of the night at an aunt's house on the other side of town.

But it soon began to seem as if no one in the town of Mattoon was safe.

The newspapers would report that the Kearneys were the first victims of the "Anesthetic Prowler" and assumed it was a robbery. But Aline and her daughter were not the first to encounter the "prowler" - he had struck two days earlier, at two houses in another part of town.

And the Kearney home would not be the last he would visit in Mattoon. Within days, a hysteria would grip the city, and dozens of reports would pour in, eventually getting the attention of even the FBI.

Who was the mysterious man spraying gas into the windows of unassuming residents of the small Illinois town?

That answer may be as complicated as the identity of the hundreds of other mysterious figures that have wreaked havoc in America since the days of colonial settlement. Our history is filled with strange accounts of phantom attackers, mysterious beings, and inexplicable assault.

Many of these figures seem to make their presence known in an area for a time and then vanish without a trace, leaving no clue as to their purpose or why they committed the strange acts that they did. Are they fiction or truth? Solid or supernatural? Human or otherworldly? Do they enter our existence from somewhere else, then simply step back to their own time and place and leave ours forever? Or could they be easier to explain? Are they merely odd loners with a penchant for science, a prank gone wrong, or a clever hoaxer intent on preserving their identity?

No one can say - but whoever these weird apparitions might be, they have left an indelible mark on the haunted landscape of America and have become a part of our strange history that few are familiar with.

This will be a book like no other you have read before. It offers no easy answers or simple solutions. It's not a mystery that can be solved. But it will have you wondering where the next "sinister stranger" might appear. And whether one of these "phantom attacks" could happen to you.

The answer is possibly...

If it can happen to the people in this book, it can happen to anyone. If that doesn't convince you to keep the lights on at night, I'm not sure what will.

1. AMERICA'S BLACK GHOSTS

A Black ghost.
A black ghost with a huge dagger sunk to the hilt in its bosom is reported from New Castle, Indiana.
**Richmond Climax (Richmond, Kentucky)
July 23, 1890**

The phenomenon of the "Black Ghost" seems to be strictly an American anomaly. Yes, there are stories "ladies in black," and spirits in black robes told in Europe and around the world, but the sinister strangers that appear in this chapter seem to be something else altogether.

For the most part, they aren't haunting a particular location, and they come and go with no explanation. At times, they seem to be flesh and blood, especially when they commit acts of violence, and yet, they vanish like the wind. Solid objects pass through them, and, often, they glide about as though they aren't bound to the earth by gravity as the rest of us are.

So, what are these creatures?

I have absolutely no idea. They all seem to be something different yet have so many similarities that various accounts from all over America feature many identical details. Their appearance is nearly the same - right down to the black shape and often towering height - as is their penchant for frightening unsuspecting people in the darkness. And yet, the peak of the Black Ghost sightings occurred in the late nineteenth century and early twentieth century, making it nearly impossible for witnesses to compare notes about the creatures with people on the other side of the country.

Sightings of the Black Ghosts multiplied around the turn of the last century and then slowly faded away until nothing was heard about them anymore. The newspaper accounts of the era helped to stoke a near-hysteria among the people where the sightings took place. Yet, a few years later, the stories would be dismissed as folklore, even though no solution to the mystery of these creatures was ever found.

Flesh and blood attackers or supernatural denizens of the other world? I'll present the evidence of their presence, and you can decide for yourself. Just don't be too quick to doubt their existence - people were undoubtedly encountering *something* in cities and small towns across America in those days.

What that *something* was, though, is still a mystery.

DECATUR, ILLINOIS - 1881

One of the first accounts of a so-called "Black Ghost" I was able to find dates to January 1881. It turned out to be a peculiar flurry of sightings for two reasons. The first was that it would be another decade before Black Ghost sightings and attacks began to occur regularly across the country. They would then continue on and off for the next 20 years until abruptly coming to an end - in this form anyway.

The other thing that makes the 1881 sightings so strange is that another spurt of Black Ghost sightings would occur in this same town in 1903. Was it the same figure or something else altogether?

The 1881 Decatur encounters didn't get a lot of press - that dramatically changed in 1903 - and were skewed to poke fun at the "colored citizens" who reported the attacks. The two news articles that appeared one week apart were filled with racial slurs to emphasize the superstitious nature of local African Americans.

The articles don't make clear the dates when the sightings began, only that it was a week or so before the first one, which appeared on January 1. The first reported witness - who had his "eyes starting from his sockets" was a "colored man" who was walking home past the African Methodist Episcopal Church when he saw a huge, dark object. He described it as having the general shape of gigantic armless and headless man - a black mass that moved swiftly in his direction, although it was gliding, not walking. The man "let out a howl" and began running for home.

Another witness, Mrs. Gray, who lived in a "hollow" near the church on the city's south side, reported that she heard a knocking sound on her door one night, and when she opened it, she saw the black shape. The creature retreated from the light coming from the house, seemed to fall down, and disappeared. She was horrified, she said, and quickly slammed the door.

Charley Stains and John Moreland were walking home with their dates following a holiday party when they saw the apparition. They were allegedly so frightened that they fled the street, leaving the two young women they had been accompanying behind.

The story spread, and while most of the black community didn't believe it at first, they soon changed their mind when the list of people who had seen the Black Ghost grew to include respected African Americans like Stanton Fields, James Williams, and, specifically, Hue Singleton, the first black business owner in the city.

More reports followed. A young boy claimed the ghost followed him when he went outside to gather wood but vanished just past a nearby cemetery fence. Julia Banister stated that her sighting of the ghost nearly caused her to faint, and she was sick for days afterward.

The excitement reached such a point that men armed with pistols and clubs began patrolling the streets near the A.M.E Church each night around midnight, hoping to track down the monster. The police were also searching, although they believed the Black Ghost was not a ghost at all. They pointed to a recent rash of chicken thefts as evidence that the spirit was a material being.

Whatever it was, it was already gone.

In a follow-up article published on January 8, the newspaper expressed the disappointment of the searchers who had waited for the ghost to return in the cold early morning hours. After only a few nights of close encounters, the Black Ghost was gone.

But the creature - or something an awful lot like him - would return in just two decades.

BROOKLYN, NEW YORK – 1893

There was only one report about a Black Ghost in Brooklyn in November 1893. Although the local newspaper does state that witnesses "looked across the street and saw the big figure in black - which they immediately concluded was the ghost they had heard so much about." Wherever they'd heard about it, it had not been in the newspapers of the time.

According to this article, though, people of the neighborhood began reporting the ghost around mid-November 1893. It had been seen several times, but few witnesses had come forward publicly to say that they had seen it appear. Two of them were Frederick Beadle and his brother, Charles.

Eastern Park Baseball fields in Brooklyn in the 1890s. It was near the park when the Black Ghost was encountered.

Beadle worked at the Eastern Park baseball fields and was walking home from work with his brother on Sunday, November 26, at around 9:00 p.m. They had started walking along Jerome Street when they spotted the Black Ghost. They said that it was dancing up and down, with its arms extended, in front of a young woman who was apparently struck dumb with terror.

The Beadles let out a shout and sprinted across the street in the direction of the confrontation. The ghost heard their approach, stopped its antics, and darted away from them into the shadows. Both men swore that it vaulted over a high farm fence with ease, but when it did, they became convinced that it was wearing pants under its black shroud.

Was it a hoax? If it was, it didn't matter to the young woman they had rescued. She was badly frightened by the encounter, which, as far as I can tell, was the last time it was seen in Brooklyn.

PEORIA, ILLINOIS - 1897

In July 1897, the "colored" section of town was in the Peoria newspaper when reports began coming in about a Black Ghost that was spotted on the north side of the city. Once again, writers poked fun at African Americans and their superstitions, suggesting that children were in bed early at night and black men were making fewer trips to lodges and clubs with the ghost on the prowl. They "prefer to be tired in the evenings and stay strictly at home," the newspaper wrote.

The sightings had started in late June when locals began reporting a "strange black object" that wandered around at night, chasing people who ventured out into the dark streets and alleyways.

Some blamed the appearance of the Black Ghost on a neighborhood death that had occurred about three months earlier, and "many residents - reputable people - are firmly convinced that it is the ghost of the dead come back to earth to either worry its enemies or else that it is dissatisfied."

Whatever the source of the spirit, it spent more than a week roaming the streets, following those who walked alone until they finally fled for their lives.

And then, as with every other incident of this type, the Black Ghost simply disappeared and was never heard from again.

Well, not in Peoria anyway.

BOONVILLE, INDIANA - 1897

On November 28, 1897, the *Chicago Chronicle* reported that the residents of Boonville - a small town just east of Evansville in the far southern part of the state - had been frightened for nearly a week by encounters with a Black Ghost. "It has been suddenly appearing at the side of men and women, and after

Downtown Boonville in the 1890s

accompanying them a short distance, or until the approach of another person, it vanishes," the paper reported.

These encounters had been reported to the town marshal, and while he claimed to have tried to capture the figure, it had never appeared for him. And even if it had, there is little he could have charged it with, even if it had been a flesh and blood person. The figure never threatened anyone. As the newspaper stated, it would only be "silently sociable, an escort for women and a companion for men."

But that didn't make it less unnerving.

A week before the article, a young woman was walking down the street and passed an alley in an upscale part of town. From out of the shadows, the Black Ghost appeared and lurched out of the alley. It was very tall, she later said, and awkward in its movements. But it was very quick and absolutely noiseless. It was all in black, with a loose, flowing cloak and a hood pulled up over its head. The ghost came right up to her as she walked and matched her pace down the street.

At first, she was startled but then assumed it must be a practical joke of some kind. She tried speaking to the figure, but there was no reply - and no sound. She realized that she could hear the clack of her footsteps on the brick street, but the ghost was still silent.

And that's when she decided to run.

She had been on her way to a nearby friend's house, and thinking she might escape from the unwelcome escort by running, she ran faster than she had ever run in her life, she later recalled. But the ghost easily kept pace with her. When she ran through the gate of her friend's home, though, the ghost vanished.

She didn't see it leave. When her friend opened the front door, she collapsed inside in a heap fainted dead away.

Another encounter occurred the following night. This time, it appeared to a man who was walking in the same neighborhood. He later said he didn't see it arrive but became aware of its presence as it suddenly began keeping pace with him. His description of it matched that of others who had seen it - tall, black robe, hood, and completely silent.

The man had heard about other sightings of the figure, so he decided to try something that no one else had done - he decided to ignore it. As he walked along, staring straight ahead, it was as though the ghost realized what he was doing. It began flitting all around him, appearing on one side of him, then the other. It kept pace with the man, even when traveling along directly in front of him.

When the man finally arrived at his gate, the ghost disappeared. "Although the gentleman says he was on the alert for that action," the newspaper concluded, "he cannot tell what became of his ghostly companion."

Whatever this figure was, it left Boonville a short time later, and no further sightings occurred.

COLD SPRINGS, NEW YORK - 1900

In early December 1900, a Black Ghost made at least two appearances in the village of Cold Springs on Long Island.

A woman who lived on Main Street was the first resident to spot the apparition, claiming that she had seen a large figure in black gliding up the street one evening. It vanished before she could get a good look at it.

Soon after this, W.J. Jones, an oyster shipper, went to the docks around 4:00 a.m. because he believed that someone was stealing his oysters. After failing to find the thieves, he started walking home - until something huge and black came up in front of him. It was shrouded all in black, but Jones said it was vaguely shaped like a woman.

Jones sprang back away from the ghost, and as he did so, the figure turned and glided away from him along Main Street. Jones followed at a distance, but when he turned around because he thought he heard someone behind him and then looked back, the figure had vanished.

As far as I know, it was never seen again.

CHILLICOTHE, OHIO - 1901

In January 1901, a Black Ghost began terrorizing residents of the East End of Chillicothe, walking up and down Watts Street and South Main, clad in a heavy black robe. Several people attempted to get a look at the figure's face, but it was covered with a heavy veil.

In addition to neighborhood residents, the ghost was spotted many times by the men from Firehouse Station No. 3. Charles Mallow and Bill Matthews, two firefighters on duty during the late-night hours, told a reporter from the *Chillicothe Gazette* that they would "find more enjoyment in life" if the ghost would go somewhere else.

The sightings went on for more than a week - and some were more disconcerting than others. Two of railroad conductor Mel Eveland's children spotted the unnerving shape and were so frightened that they ran into a neighbor's house for safety. The entire district was living in fear, and the police put out warnings for the "man or woman" pretending to be a ghost - they would be caught and exposed.

But they never were.

One of the last incidents occurred around January 19, when a Mrs. Willis, who resided in the East End, was walking home from a friend's house around 9:00 p.m. She was standing at the corner of Main and Watts Streets when a man approached her and said hello.

Mrs. Willis didn't reply.

The man turned to her and said, "If you won't speak to me, I'll make you speak."

This threat frightened the woman so much that she ran back to her friend's house and frantically beat on the door until she was let inside. Had she run to the fire station, a short distance from where she had been approached, she would have found protection, but she was too badly scared to think of going anywhere else.

The unknown man who accosted her was no ghost. He was described as wearing a cap, a light overcoat, and having a light mustache.

The firefighters from Station No. 3 searched for the man but had no luck. They believed he was looking for the Black Ghost and mistook Mrs. Willis for an imposter.

WHERE IS THE BLACK GHOST? NO ONE KNOWS

What has become of the black ghost?

If this question is heard once it is heard fifty times a day, but there is no answer. No one knows. Some think it has been scared away by the crowds that gathered nightly to see it, but this is not plausible—ghosts never get scared. Others think there never was one. The latter seems to be the popular opinion.

A report has been in circulation for two or three days to the effect that a woman, residing in the neighborhood of Minnich avenue, the haunted spot, had been caught impersonating the disembodied soul, but this report is absolutely false. The police, who were supposed to have found the wo

She was wearing a long black coat at the time.

NEAR BUTTE, MONTANA – 1901

A Black Ghost began making nightly visits to the small town of Centerville - not far from Butte -- in early March 1901. The visits became brushes with terror for many of the residents who encountered the creature on the dark streets. And these were not merely sightings. Some of the residents were not only badly frightened by the mysterious figure, but some were also attacked and badly beaten, like two young boys who encountered the Black Ghost on March 11.

The descriptions of the figure were always the same. It was very large and clothed from head to toe in a black robe. It seemed to appear from nowhere out of the shadows and loom over unsuspecting people who were walking past. One newspaper report stated that the ghost was easily found by those who walked the streets late at night. "Usually, they are able to get a glimpse of it," the article claimed.

On March 10, two men came to Centerville from Butte to try and track down the figure. Will Smeltzer from Leadville, Colorado, visiting a local friend, Will Osborn, heard about the ghost sightings and wanted to see things for himself. They arrived in town and roamed the streets until nearly midnight when they got a glimpse of a shape all in black that emerged from behind a rock near a bridge.

The ghost was only a few yards away, and they could see it distinctly. It appeared to be a tall, thin figure draped in a black robe. The description is the same as similar apparitions from around the country, with one exception - they said that when it threw its arms up, a phosphorescent light appeared at the place where its head and face should be.

The young men turned and ran for their lives.

At that same moment, the ghost let out an inhuman shriek, and Smeltzer took a tumble at the sound of it. He later said it

Centerville, Montana in the early 1900s

"curdled his blood." He stumbled and fell, skinning his nose, and cutting his face badly in several places.

It was the last that either of the men wanted to see the Black Ghost, but others in town didn't share that opinion. Groups gathered every night - usually well-armed groups - who patrolled the streets, looking for the figure to return. Most of them were local miners who, after a few rounds at the saloon, promised to track down the ghost and "fill it full of lead."

One of the groups that ventured out on the night of March 12 comprised Chief of Police Lavelle, Captain Leyden, Detective Murphy, Jailer McGlynn, and the station's bulldog mascot. They headed out armed with shotguns that had been loaded with rock salt. If they missed, they told a reporter from the *Anaconda Standard*, they were depending on the bulldog to bite the creature.

We never learned how the law and order contingent fared that night, but subsequent articles chronicled the fates of 10 or 12 young men who went looking for the Black Ghost on East

Summit Street, near the Mountain Consolidated Mine. The ghost has been spotted several times in that neighborhood, always vanishing near an old, abandoned house.

Around midnight, the men began surveilling the house and waiting for the ghost to appear. Unfortunately for them, it approached from behind, let out an "unearthly wail," and sent all the men running, except for two, who stayed behind, crouched behind some rocks. After the figure left, they decided to go into the abandoned house and see if they could discover the creature's lair.

And they didn't come back out again - not under their own power anyway.

After the two men didn't rejoin their companions, it was decided to break into the house to rescue them. Once inside, they found their friends unconscious on the floor. Both appeared to have been badly beaten. They carried them outside and got as far away from the house as possible before trying to rouse the two injured men. When they were revived, the men said they had been surprised in the house by the spook. The figure had raised the veil that covered its face, and all they could recall were two burning, luminous balls in place of its eyes. The ghost shrieked again and struck both men with a tremendous blow that sent them spinning to the floor.

Two days later, the Black Ghost was in the papers again, this time with an account of a party of five men who tracked the creature and shot at it.

On March 13, 1901, three men - Tom Walsh, Mike Collane, and Jack Murphy - were joined by two newspaper reporters as they searched for the ghost in Centerville. The search began along the Butte, Anaconda, and Pacific Railroad tracks, nearing a pumping station on Main Street. Around 12.45 a.m., they split up with Walsh and the reporters going north on the tracks, walking next to a row of freight cars that were standing on the rails. Collane and Murphy went west, traveling under the Main Street bridge.

Minutes passed, and soon Collane and Murphy reached the end of the cut and walked into an open space that was now covered with snow and ice. Just then, the black figure emerged from the darkness on the south side of the tracks and came rushing toward them. It didn't walk or run; the men were sure of that - the figure was gliding straight at them over the rough terrain.

When the figure was only six feet away from them, Murphy raised his handgun and ordered the ghost to stop. In response, the creature was suddenly "illuminated." According to the newspaper story, "On its bosom there appeared a light as though produced by electricity, and the eyes of the object were as large as balls of fire. The face itself was luminous and had a bluish-yellow cast - intensely sepulchral, and when it stretched out its hands, they became luminous, too, and appeared transparent."

And that's when Murphy shot it.

When the bullet hit the ghost, it darted to the side of the cut, and its lights went out immediately. In a moment, it appeared again on the side of the hill, its black shape plainly visible against the backdrop of the snow. Its luminous glow returned a moment later, and both Murphy and Collane opened fire at it. They then said it "disappeared across the open stretch like a streak of lightning."

After hearing the shots, Walsh and the two reporters ran to the scene, and Collane and Murphy told them what had happened. Both swore the creature had been no more than 10 feet away when they emptied their revolvers into it. Whatever this thing was, the bullets hadn't even fazed it.

The two men were agitated but returned to the search for the Black Ghost - or even for its footprints in the snow - but, as the reporters vouched, there was no sign that it had ever been there.

The writer of the newspaper article had the last say about this incident. He wrote, "If the apparition or ghost, or whatever the object was that was encountered on the railroad tracks last night is not supernatural, it is certainly one of the most puzzling things which have ever come up for discussion in Butte. There is no question that the appearance of the object was not a creation in the minds of the men who went in search of it, and if it had been a man, it could not have survived the shots which were taken at it from a distance of less than ten feet by two good marksmen."

This was not the last sighting of the Black Ghost in the area. A few weeks later, near the end of the month, it turned up again, but this time in Walkerville, a nearby town. According to witnesses, who reported the sightings to the town marshal, the ghost had been seen around the old Lexington mine and mill, which had been long abandoned. One witness saw it near the mill's crumbling smokestacks, while several others claimed it appeared from the mine entrance around midnight.

The first person to see it was a man who burst into a Walkerville saloon, ranting about his close encounter with the black-robed figure. Others in the saloon agreed that the man had not been drinking and professed to accept his story as truth.

This began a new round of hunts for the ghost. One party of young men went out looking. When they reached the town's schoolhouse, they fled, all claiming the creature was lurking behind a wall.

It wasn't.

It was Marshal Kennedy, the town's top lawman, who had gone up the hill to the schoolhouse during his own search for the figure.

The excitement over the apparition lasted for a few more nights and then faded away. Apparently, whatever it was, it had vanished and left Montana behind.

BUSHNELL, ILLINOIS – 1902

Starting in early March 1902, the residents of this small Illinois town began to be disturbed by a sinister figure in black that was walking their streets. Described as wearing a long black robe with a heavy mourning veil over its face, this Black Ghost was spotted on different streets in town and at no particular time – although always lurking after dark.

In most cases, the shape simply appeared on the street, emerging from behind trees or alleyways, providing a jolt of fear to anyone walking in its direction. But then, on two or three occasions, it gave chase, and the frightened people who encountered it said it was "with only the fleetest running that they have been able to keep out of the way."

On one occasion, an attempt was made to capture the spirit, but after a pursuit of several blocks, the figure disappeared, and the hunt was abandoned.

The sightings continued for just over a week and then suddenly came to a stop. The Black Ghost had mysteriously vanished, but its lingering memory served to keep a great many men, women, and children off the streets at night for some months to come.

TOLEDO, OHIO – 1902

The "Black Ghost of Toledo," as the newspapers called it, may be something outside the realm of most of the other Black Ghosts in this chapter – and yet, familiar to the other "sinister strangers" in this book.

I'm not sure there was any point during the brief flurry of Black Ghost sightings in Toledo in November 1902 that the authorities believed it was a supernatural creature. For more than three weeks, people on the east side of the town believed the black-robed creature was a man in disguise - a man who was attempting to kidnap children.

Whoever he was, he desperately tried to grab children and carry them off, causing mothers to keep their sons and daughter at home. Men on the east side armed themselves and arranged patrols to keep an eye out for the figure in black.

Finally, on the morning of November 30, a 12-year-old named Johnny Barror was riding his bicycle when he was snatched off it by the figure and told that he would be instantly killed if he raised an alarm. As the Black Ghost tried to carry the boy away, Johnny struggled his way loose and ran away down the street. He sprinted for nearly two blocks before running into two police officers. They hurried back to the scene of the attack and recovered the boy's bicycle, but the attacker was gone.

This attempted abduction turned out to be the figure's last. Whoever the man was, he vanished after that and didn't return.

JERSEY CITY, NEW JERSEY - 1903

In early January 1903, a Black Ghost began plaguing the residents of Jersey City, appearing in the streets and accosting young women who were walking alone. Mobs of vigilantes took to the streets in pursuit, and eventually, the sightings stopped - but not before the ghost was blamed for one young woman's death.

The figure was first encountered by a young woman referred to in reports as Miss Arndt, a cashier at a general supply store. On her way home from work, she was confronted by

Jersey City around the time of the Black Ghost sightings that terrified the residents

a tall, black apparition in a robe. A heavy veil hid its face. The figure reached out and grabbed her by the arm.

"Let me go!" she shouted.

The ghost didn't reply. It dragged her bodily across the sidewalk and threw her up against a lamppost. As Miss Arndt struggled, the figure bent down and peered at her face. She could not see its eyes but felt the figure was looking straight at her. Then, it released her arm, turned, and vanished into the shadows.

Miss Arndt later told the police that the strength of the creature's grip caused her to believe it was a man in the robe, but she was unable to be sure.

On January 10, another young woman told a similar story. However, she let out a few screams when the ghost released her and began walking away. A man came running out of the darkness and asked her what was wrong. She pointed at the Black Ghost, and he chased after it. He managed to grab the figure by the arm, but before he could subdue it, the figure lashed out and hit him so hard in the chest that he went sprawling onto the sidewalk.

After that, the ghost vanished again.

In the early morning hours of January 11, the driver of a milk wagon named Edwards said that he saw the ghost on Virginia Avenue, near Bergen Avenue. Having heard about the other sightings, Edwards chased after it. He grabbed the figure by the arm, but the tall specter turned and smashed him twice in the face. As Edwards stumbled backward, the ghost calmly walked away from him and disappeared into an alley.

Meanwhile, the hunt was on for the black-robed character. Around the time of these sightings, an estimated 1,000 men and boys were patrolling the streets at night - armed with clubs, baseball bats, shovels, and knives - hoping to capture the creature. These vigilante groups roamed the downtown district and spread out through the neighborhoods, intent on finding the ghost before it terrorized anyone else.

And they weren't alone in the search. The police were out on the streets, too. The sightings - or rather, the attacks - had forced them to pay attention to what was happening in Jersey City, even if Captain Nugent and Detective James Larkin publicly expressed that they were more afraid of the vigilante committees than they were the Black Ghost. They refused to take the sightings and attacks seriously, though, and after failing to capture the ghost, they simply decided the Black Ghost had never existed at all.

The sightings? Wild imaginations? The attacks? Just a prankster trying to scare young women. Just as in many other towns and cities, it was easier for the Jersey City police to dismiss something entirely than to admit that something was occurring that was not easily explained.

The sightings of the specter became fewer and eventually stopped altogether. But the incident would end on a tragic note on February 10 with the death of 22-year-old Mary Sheehy of Jersey City. She died at City Hospital of hysteria which her doctors claimed came from her worrying over stories about the Black Ghost, told to her by fellow employees at the watch factory where she worked.

The week before her death, Mary had a breakdown at work and began refusing to go outside after dark, fearing that the ghost would catch her. She deteriorated to the point that she became obsessed with the thought that someone was chasing her. On the morning of February 7, she was taken to City Hospital, where she died a few days later.

As far as anyone could learn, Mary never had any personal experience with the black figure. She simply became obsessed with the idea of what was out there and that it was coming for her.

The idea slowly drove her insane.

DECATUR, ILLINOIS – 1903

More than two decades after the 1881 sightings of a Black Ghost, fear gripped the entire city of Decatur as people began to be terrorized by a chilling apparition in a black robe, with a veil covering its face and "awful eyes that burned like fire." It haunted the city - particularly the West Side - and soon generated a panic in Decatur like nothing that had ever occurred before.

The first sighting of the Black Ghost occurred on November 6 when a shoe repairer from the Rogers and Clark store named Edward Freemont spotted the figure outside of his home. He was walking home late and had just reached his front steps at the corner of Eldorado and Monroe Streets, near the Cumberland Presbyterian Church, when he saw the black shape appear. Freemont would later state that he heard no footsteps as it approached him. He said that the figure moved very slowly and deliberately - a kind of glide.

Edward described the form as being swathed in black from head to foot, with its face covered by some sort of veil or hood.

At the moment the apparition appeared, Mrs. Freemont stepped out of the house and saw the figure from the porch. Before either of them could call out, the shape had drifted away to the street. It slowly moved toward the church and then abruptly turned and darted north. The Freemonts hurried after the fleeing figure, but by the time they reached the street, it was empty. Both later said that no human could have gotten out of sight in the brief moments it took them to follow the shape.

On Sunday evening, November 8, the Black Ghost was spotted again. Several young ladies were walking home from church in the 200 block of West Decatur Street and saw the black shape standing in a yard a short distance from them. They believed that the specter spotted them at the same time because it looked up, darted around one corner of the house, and glided out of sight - never making a sound.

The young women remembered reading Edward Freemont's account of the shape in that morning's newspaper and recognized it from its description.

They stopped a moment and looked back and saw it looking at them from around a corner.

That's when they ran.

The next sighting occurred on Tuesday night, November 10. A young lady was walking alone along West Wood Street when the black-shrouded phantom appeared between two houses near Union Street. The shape came quickly toward her, and she began to scream. Just at that moment, a carriage drove out of a nearby barn, and the figure fled.

The young woman reported the incident to the police, who assumed, even after the other sightings, that it was nothing more than a prank. But then, more sightings began to occur on the city's West Side. The figure was reported on West Main Street, West Wood, and along Pine Street. Who, or what, this specter might be was unknown, but it terrified

A view down West Main Street in Decatur, toward the area of the city where the Black Ghost was sighted the most

people as it lurched from the shadows and then vanished without a trace.

News of the ghost quickly spread throughout the city. Sightings were reported in the newspapers, and the phantom became a heated topic of conversation in restaurants, saloons, barbershops, billiard halls, and schools. The police admitted to being perplexed by the weird sightings, and the average people in the city were intrigued -- and a little unnerved.

Two additional Black Ghost encounters took place on November 14, when dozens of people were out looking for the monster. The first occurrence took place during the early evening hours when a young man called the police from a grocery store on the West Side, claiming that he had seen the shape. Although the caller never gave his name, the authorities took the call seriously and dispatched two officers to the store. The witness left before the officers arrived, and a search of the neighborhood revealed nothing out of the ordinary.

Henry Ray, a student at Millikin University, was out that evening, having taken a streetcar from the college to a downtown theater. He stayed late, and the streetcars had stopped running before he needed to return to Millikin. Content to travel on foot, he had reached Haworth Avenue when he told police that he encountered the Black Ghost crouching in the shadows along the north side of the street. The creature appeared to have a club in its hands, and when it saw Ray walking alone, it got up and started toward him. Ray said that he first thought he would confront the ghost, but then he changed his mind and began to run south on Haworth Avenue. He claimed that the creature chased him as far as Dr. Lonergan's home on West Decatur Street and then had disappeared.

The ghost returned on November 15. Fred Travis and Dell Hooey, two young men who worked for the Chicago, Bloomington & Decatur Railroad freight house, encountered it on North Monroe Street, just north of the Cerro Gordo Street intersection. The two men were on their way home from the freight house around 8:30 p.m. They had just turned north from Cerro Gordo on the east side of Monroe and were about halfway to the railroad tracks when they met the specter. They were busy talking to one another when it appeared and startled them both.

"There it is," Dell shouted to his friend. "Let's find out what it is!"

The young men's description of the creature matched what had been reported by other witnesses. It was black from head to foot and draped in apparel like a nun, except a thick veil covered the face. Its motion was not like that of a person walking, but rather a gliding movement, as if on wheels or rollers. Fred later stated that it seemed to have a shiny object, like a fork or small rake, in its right hand. Its other arm was folded across its chest, hunching the monster's broad shoulders.

Both men gave chase to the ghost. Fred, who had recently played for a semi-professional baseball team, was regarded as one of the fastest men in the city. Regardless, the ghost easily outpaced them. Fred had been carrying a board with him, which he planned to take home and burn as kindling in his stove, but when he saw the ghost was getting away, he hurled the board at it. He was sure that if the phantom had been a material being, the board would have hit it. Instead, it passed through the ghost and fell to the sidewalk. Moments later, the specter disappeared.

It did not, both young men said, go up or down or turn to either side. It simply disappeared. It had been in plain sight until that moment.

Later that same night, a man named Theodore Fowler encountered the Black Ghost, this time on West Decatur Street. He was in the 900 block, walking east on the north side of the street at about 10:30 p.m. when he saw the black-shrouded figure appear ahead of him. It glided along for about a half-block and then abruptly vanished. This convinced him that the figure had been a ghost.

By this time, the stories of Black Ghost sightings were sweeping through the city, and the West End people, especially women and children, were terrified. Many of them were too scared to leave their homes at night, but, unfortunately, even staying indoors was not enough to protect them from visitations from the ghost.

The figure appeared at the residence of Elmer Wood at 1120 West Macon Street on November 16. Three young women from Millikin University, who were boarding at the house for the school year, were talking in the parlor. They heard a noise on the front porch, and one of them went to the door to see who was there. When she looked through the glass, she let out a bloodcurdling scream. The Black Ghost was lurking on the front porch with its veiled face pressed to the glass of the front door. At the sound of the scream, the phantom fled from the porch and went straight across the street to a house on the other side. It rattled the doorknob with great ferocity, and when the woman of the house came to the door, she saw it and ran away screaming. The black ghost vanished into the darkness.

Later that same night, Mrs. Jake Lehman was terrified by the figure near her home on West Macon Street. She had walked to a nearby store on an errand and was on her way back home when the ghost appeared from the shadows. She let out a scream, and the creature chased her all the way home. She burst through the door and fell, much to the surprise of her family. "I was so badly frightened," she later said, "that I was hardly able to tell what was the matter." Someone looked out the window and saw the Black Ghost, which hurried past the house and then disappeared.

The figure also visited the home of attorney Marshall Griffin on West Decatur Street that same night. Griffin was at church with his wife, but his sister-in-law, Mrs. Childs, was in the house with her mother. The two ladies were seated in the parlor when they heard a tapping at the window. They looked up to see a face - covered in a thick black veil or mask - staring in at them. The ladies later agreed the sight was "terrifying."

Mrs. Childs, however, was not so frightened, and she didn't chase the figure away. She picked up a huge piece of coal from the fireplace and hurled it through the window at the face, shattering the window glass.

The figure, unlike the window glass, was uninjured.

By November 17, the city was in a frantic state. Around 10:30 p.m. that night, the police received a call from the yardmaster at the east end of the Wabash Railroad yards - some of the railroad boys had cornered the ghost, he said! When the police arrived, they found that the men had captured an African American man dressed in women's clothing. He had been scaring people in the nearby neighborhood as a prank.

A short time later, another call came into police headquarters from Martin's Restaurant, where different railroad workers had caught the ghost. The department patrol wagon was quickly rerouted to Jasper Street, and officers found a large crowd outside the restaurant. The "ghost" the men had captured was an 18-year-old woman named Lulu Williams, who drunkenly insisted that she was the Black Ghost. The railroad men had found her sprawled across some nearby tracks, passed out from drinking, and in danger of being run over by a train. Captain Koeppe, who was on duty at the time, put her in a cell to sleep it off.

Another "ghost" was captured on West Decatur Street that night - an older woman who lived on the street and liked to go for evening walks. The police suggested that she refrain from her nighttime sojourns until the Black Ghost could be caught.

Plainclothes police officers were put on patrol on the West Side, looking for any sign of the ghost. They didn't track down the creature, but they did give stern words of warning to several pranksters, who thought it would be fun to dress up in a black overcoat and jump out and scare people.

Unsure of what to make of the sightings that could not be explained away, police officials dismissed the ghost as a female "morphine fiend" who went crazy when she couldn't obtain her drugs. Another suggestion that was the Black Ghost was an unnamed young man in town who liked to tell sensational stories about himself as a hero, but, upon investigation, the stories turn out to be "hot air." It was thought that this man, who fancied himself a detective, was trying out a new disguise.

These were creative theories, of course, but failed to explain the mysterious disappearances of the creature or how a board could be thrown at the "morphine fiend" or the amateur detective and have it pass through either of them as if through thin air.

The people of Decatur were convinced that a real ghost was in their midst, and search parties were organized to try and track the monster down. Early in the evenings, crowds of men and boys could be found in every part of the West End. Eldorado and Monroe streets were thoroughly searched. All the search parties went armed with sticks and clubs, apparently hoping to thrash the ghost if they managed to catch it. They roamed the streets and alleys for most of the night, shouting and laughing with one another. The only thing these "ghost hunters" managed to find was trouble since residents attempting to sleep began reporting their behavior to the police around midnight.

One hunting party, organized by Earle Dodd and 12 or 15 other young men, claimed that they managed to see the ghost, but it got away. They expressed disappointment about not being able to give the figure a "thrashing."

But not every ghost hunting party was made up of local ruffians and teenagers. Dr. L.E. Conradt and about 20 members of the respected Iroquois Club took up the search for the Black Ghost. They armed themselves with clubs and went all over the West Side of town, looking behind signs, along fence rows, in orchards, and down alleys. They searched for more than two hours but could not find anything that resembled the ghost.

No additional sightings of the black ghost occurred on November 18, although the search parties were still out on the hunt. The people of Decatur remained on edge, and women were still terrified. In fact, they were so scared that talk of the ghost was blamed when two women almost burned themselves to death. A Mrs. M.M. McDonald of Stonington was spending the night of November 18 with her friend, Mrs. Gates, who lived at 531 North Monroe Street. The ladies were alone in the house, reading about the ghost sightings in the newspaper and talking about the mysterious creature, and had become very nervous by bedtime. When they retired, they placed a lighted lamp on a chair beside the bed so that they could see which way to run in case the ghost decided to call during the night.

Around 2:00 a.m., Mrs. McDonald awoke and found that her nightdress was on fire. The lamp had somehow tipped over and had set fire to the sheets. She screamed and awoke Mrs. Gates, who managed to get her into the bathroom, soak her with water, and put out the fire. Her friend's sleeve had been burned away, and her arm was badly scorched. Meanwhile, the bed itself was still on fire, and Mrs. Gates managed to wrestle the bed covers into the bathtub and extinguish the flames. The fire department was summoned, but the blaze was already out. Dr. F.M. Anderson arrived to care for Mrs. McDonald's wounds and pronounced that both women were very lucky.

Of course, the whole incident was blamed on the Black Ghost.

The ghost might have been at the Gates house in spirit, so to speak, but it was certainly not making its presence known anywhere else. After the rash of ghost hunting parties, which started on November 17, no sightings of the ghost were ever reported again. Whoever, or whatever, the creature had been, it had apparently left Decatur for good, never to return. The excitement over the "ghost attacks" subsided and the wandering gangs of ghost hunters soon found other things to do. Eventually, the panic was largely forgotten.

ST. JOSEPH, MISSOURI – 1909

Appearances of a Black Ghost on the South Side of St. Joseph, Missouri, were reported starting in early April 1909. A black-robed apparition began showing up in the Hyde Valley district at "uncanny hours" and followed residents returning home late at night. It caused such a sensation in the neighborhood the newspaper reported that a concerted effort was being made to round up and discover the identity of the figure.

Needless to say, that never happened - although this is one case in which a conclusion was reached, even if it's very hard to believe.

The sightings continued for the next week, and while the shape occasionally followed couples, it seemed to primarily target young men who had escorted their dates to their front doors and then left to walk home alone. Things became so bad around Grant and West Valley Streets that men were afraid to be out alone after dark.

According to an account about a young man that lived near the stockyards, he was followed by the black shape one night and started running to get away from it. The ghost pursued him for several blocks, both running at full speed, but the man got away by boarding a late-running streetcar.

The Black Ghost continued to appear throughout the month of April, darting around dark corners, appearing on lonely streets, and tapping on doors and windows. The police paid little attention to the reports from the South Side, so residents took it upon themselves to try and hunt down the figure.

One night, a group of "ghost hunters" tracked the shape to the vicinity of King Hill Road and Alabama Street and gave chase. They were apparently gaining on the specter when it suddenly disappeared - as one man said, "as though swallowed by the earth." It had vanished near the bridge across Brown Creek, just south of the city limits.

Another account followed a young man chased by the ghost until the fellow ran out of breath and suddenly stopped in his tracks. He bent down and picked up a large piece of brick on the side of the roads and proceeded to hurl it at his pursuer. He swore the brick passed through the creature before it scampered off to safety.

The sightings and pursuits continued for the next two weeks and then abruptly came to an end. As with all the other cities and towns where Black Ghost visitations had occurred, the figure in St. Joseph departed for no apparent reason and left a mystery behind.

The attacks had been unsolved - no matter what the local newspaper would have its readers believe.

On May 12, 1909, the *St. Joseph Gazette* ran a story about a South Side man who was on his way to visit his girlfriend when he spotted the Black Ghost at the intersection of King Hill Road and Alabama Street. Forgetting about the young woman waiting for him, he rounded up several friends and returned to the crossroads with pistols and shotguns. The ghost was still standing near a small pond, and the men opened fire on it. Bullets slammed into the creature, but it never fell, moved, or surrendered. When the men came up on it, they found this Black Ghost had been nothing more than a wooden dummy, draped in a black robe, all along.

The "South End Bugaboo was Finally Laid Out," the newspaper assured its readers. There had never been anything to fear - the ghost had never been real.

The article failed to explain the dozens of people who had been chased by the figure or encountered it in places other than King Hill Road, but it did satisfy the police and the people who had never believed in the monster to start with.

The Black Ghost sightings in St. Joseph had been "solved."

GRANTS PASS, OREGON – 1911

As much as I wish that I could offer a full accounting of this story from August 1911, records are woefully few about what must have been a time of excitement in the town of Grants Pass,

Oregon. There are few news clippings and no other written records about the "Black Ghost of Grants Pass."

The only real record that I could find - other than one clipping that said nothing more than "Grants Pass is having a ghost scare" - was printed two weeks after the last sighting of the ghost had taken place. The article noted that the figure began appearing in town around midnight in early August. It was described as a shape all in black robes, wearing a heavy black veil, but, in this case, standing more than seven feet tall.

When anyone tried to get too close to the figure, it would run away. Several people who chased after it claimed that it fled to the nearby Rogue River, climbed the high steel bridge there, and then leaped off it with a loud shriek, plunging below the water without a splash or a ripple on the surface.

The sightings occurred every night for more than a week. It appeared all over town, often in different parts of town on the same night. The newspaper noted that so many well-known citizens of Grants Pass had seen the Black Ghost that "no one doubts its existence." At first, city officials and police officers were noncommittal about the specters. Still, as eyewitnesses became more numerous, they began setting up patrols to try and capture the fiend, although all of them proved unsuccessful. The only thing that city leaders managed to do was allow "no hint" of the story to make it to "outside papers," thus ensuring that the end of this particular story would never be known.

NEW PHILADELPHIA, OHIO - 1914

Sightings of a large figure draped all in black and wearing a heavy veil began to be reported in New Philadelphia in early March of 1914.

The first person to spot the Black Ghost was a young man who lived on Fifth Street. He was walking home late and spotted the figure on Minnich Avenue - where the sightings would be centered - between Fifth Street and Broadway. As he neared the shape, he vividly recalled that it was "emitting moans and ghoulish, fiendish cries." That was all he remembered. The next thing he recalled; he was under his blankets in bed at home.

A short time later, another man claimed that he was chased by the figure. More sightings followed, and all were basically the same - a tall, cadaverous figure in a flowing black robe with a face that was shrouded by a thick, black veil. It never left the neighborhood around Minnich Avenue and the alleys between Poplar and Park Streets. It was, as the newspaper noted, "a dismal section of the city."

It was always seen at the same time every night and always at the hours just after midnight. And those who saw it? They swore you could see through it.

On the night of March 5, 1914, after hearing the stories of the ghost, five young men decided to try and capture it. Just before midnight, they went down to Minnich Avenue and devised a plan - two would approach from one direction, two more from another, and the fifth man would assist whichever pair toward which the ghost fled. They waited for more than an hour, but the Black Ghost didn't appear. Had it somehow become aware of their plan, or perhaps saw them hiding, waiting to spring the trap?

Another newspaper story noted: "What the Black Ghost is, is not known. Many persons, reliable persons, who have not touched a drop, have sworn they saw the specter stalking around the neighborhood, with arms outspread, uttering hideous noises.

"The Black Ghost is the main topic of conversation in the city, and all are anxiously waiting for someone to ferret out the mystery of the nightly appearances of the spiritual form."

A few nights after the failed attempt to capture the ghost, another, much larger, ghost hunting party set out for Minnich Avenue. More than 50 boys from the local high school were determined to investigate it. They arrived just before midnight, spread out in hiding down the street, and quietly waited for the figure to appear.

But the ghost thwarted these efforts, too. It seemed to only want an audience of one.

The police also began to set up patrols of the neighborhood. They were either searching for the Black Ghost or were attempting to run off the crowds that were now roaming the streets in the vicinity of Minnich Avenue each night. But all the police officers managed to do was scare away everyone, including the ghost.

After March 11, the Black Ghost was never seen in New Philadelphia again.

"WOMEN IN BLACK" AND OMENS OF DOOM

The mysterious "Black Ghosts" that were so prevalent across the country in the late nineteenth and early twentieth centuries were not the only sinister strangers to wreak havoc on small towns and large. These strange shapes seemed to have no purpose. They came and went, walked, and floated, chased after unsuspecting witnesses, and usually just stood looming over a street corner somewhere, waiting for someone to notice them and get scared.

But the Black Ghosts had cousins of a sort. These "cousins" were almost always female, and they usually seemed to have a message to deliver to the living - a warning that something terrible was about to happen.

The "banshee" was the feminine death omen spirit of Ireland and Scotland and manifested to warn of an approaching death in the family to which it was attached.

Our American "banshees" are not so formal and have little use for individual families. Their appearances are much more random, often wreaking havoc in a town or a place for a short time or are connected to a place where tragedy often occurs.

CHICAGO - 1890s

For years, stories swirled about the intersection of Chicago and Western Avenues in the city or, more specifically, about the electric trolley cars that drove around this corner. There was, the stories said, a figure in black that appeared at this spot in the wake of an accidental death.

Sergeant Stephen Tarnoski of the West Chicago Avenue police station is one of the few men who could vouch for the existence of this specter. The figure that was seen appeared to be that of a woman in mourning clothes, draped in black, with a heavy black veil covering her face.

Trolley cars on West Chicago Avenue in the 1890s – around the time of the ominous sightings

The area around the police station was already known for ghost sightings. There were stories of a woman who clung to the trolley pole of a car that ran her down, killing her instantly. Several people, including the motorman and conductor of the car, had told Sergeant Tarnoski of this apparition, but he had not seen it himself.

Of the ghost in black, though, he could speak from experience.

The officer got a look at the phantom in November 1896, when a little girl was killed by the State Street trolley car at Division and Clark Streets. The sergeant had often heard about the spirit showing itself at the Chicago and Western Avenue crossing, and each time the sergeant noted that someone had been killed by the electric cars that day.

On the day the little girl was killed, Sergeant Tarnoski started for his station at 4:30 p.m. and came to Chicago and Western Avenues just 15 minutes later. He had not, until that time, believed the stories of the ghost, but as he waited for his connecting car, he saw something moving in the center of the tracks,

He saw a human form rise out of the solid ground, draped in black. Black as midnight, the thing could be plainly seen against the gray of the murky day. The sergeant was fascinated and stood still and watched the figure. It began swaying back and forth and then swung its hands and arms as if in some incantation or prayer. Up and down and about, the arms swung, and the sergeant realized he was watching some sort of spectral ritual.

Then the figure began to fade away, and, in a minute, the eastbound car came up to his stop with a clanging bell and the roar of wheels.

By then, the shape was gone.

How long this "death omen" appeared at Chicago and Western Avenues remains unknown. I have written quite a lot about the city over the years and, even though I have found a lot of first-hand accounts of the supernatural from police officers, I had never heard this story before. But I would imagine when the city of Chicago stopped using trolley cars, the strange supplications of the figure in black finally came to an end.

CARBONDALE, PENNSYLVANIA – 1892

Members of mining families in northwestern Pennsylvania - most of them European immigrants - became unsettled in February of 1892 when stories of a woman in black began circulating among them. The stories claimed the woman was seen in a black dress and heavy veil, appearing just after midnight, in various sections of town.

The residents were especially unsettled because the woman had visited the region many times over the years. Each time she appeared; they knew it meant one thing - a calamity would occur.

The woman was first seen in 1892 by a "caller" for the Erie Railroad. A caller was the man whose duty was to awaken the miners who went out on the trains in the morning. He said that the woman in black was standing in the street near the railroad depot. As he walked toward her, she moved off slowly in the opposite direction. The caller and another railroad employee, puzzled as to why a woman would be out in such a lonely part of town at such a late hour, decided to go and speak to her. But as they got closer, she continued to move away. They picked up the pace, walking rapidly at first but then started to sprint, but they could not overtake the woman. She always stayed a few yards in front of them. When they called out to her, she didn't respond. Strangest of all, she didn't seem to be in a hurry. Her movements were slow and unhurried, yet they could not catch up to her. When they finally gave up the chase, she vanished into the shadows.

A few nights later, she showed up in a different part of the city and led two other men in a similarly strange chase, also disappearing into the darkness.

During the early morning hours of Friday, February 12, she was spotted again. This time, she disappeared under the same mysterious circumstances near the entrance to the old Coal Brook mine entrance.

When word spread of this, men who had been employed at the mine for years refused to show up for work on Saturday. Most of the employees were Italian immigrants, and while their refusal to work was dismissed as nothing more than "superstition," it seemed they had good reason to be afraid.

The woman in black had been seen before and had brought death and terror with her each time.

Miners stated that nearly 50 years before, the same woman - or one just like her - began to be seen prowling about the town. Soon after she appeared on the morning of February 5, 1846, an immense section of slate fell from the roof of one of the Delaware & Hudson Canal Company mines. About 150 men were working in the mine at the time. Those in other sections escaped safely, but 15 men working under the ceiling that collapsed were killed instantly - or were trapped and unable to be rescued. Those who didn't die immediately starved to death in the darkness.

In the winter of 1864, talk spread through the neighborhoods where the miners lived about sightings of the mysterious woman in black. Years had passed, but those who recognized her claimed that she looked exactly as she had nearly two decades earlier.

Within a week of the appearances of the spirit, a cholera epidemic broke out in Carbondale and spread around the region. This was a period when how cholera was spread was denied by the authorities. In general, cholera was blamed on dirty living conditions, especially those of poor immigrants, which most of the miners were.

But this was not the case. It had everything to do with the causal sanitation methods of the time. Drinking water was either dipped or pumped from shallow dug wells, rivers, or lakes. Individual households deposited sewage in streams or cesspools, and they were allowed to overflow or seep into the water sources. To make matters worse, water sources and sewage disposal were positioned for convenience, not safety - often so close together that the odor and taste of drinking water was a problem.

But that was science for the future. In the 1860s, the religion of the immigrants - usually Catholic, Russian, or Greek Orthodox

- was seen as troublesome. Many blamed the epidemic on the sinful behavior of the miners and their families or the wrath of an angry God.

The miners didn't know who, or what, to blame. They only knew they had been warned by the woman in black.

In the spring of 1872, she came back. Once again, reports circulated of the woman in black roaming the streets of Carbondale and other nearby communities. Miners all over the region began to fear that something terrible was about to happen.

The woman in black was right again.

On April 2, 1872, the Lackawanna breaker, located a half-mile from Carbondale, and owned by the Delaware and Hudson Coal Company, collapsed in a terrible wind gust, carrying both men and mine cars into the chasm below it.

A coal breaker was a plant built outside of the mine itself, where coal was broken into pieces and then sorted into categories of uniform size. The plant also removed impurities from the coal - like slate or rock - and then graded the coal on the percent of impurities that remained. The sorting by size was particularly important for anthracite coal, which required air to flow around it evenly to burn efficiently.

Anthracite coal breakers were very labor-intensive. The removal of impurities was done by hand, usually by boys between 8 and 12 years old, referred to as "breaker boys." That sat on wooden seats, perched over chutes and conveyor belts, plucking slate and other impurities out of the coal that flowed beneath them. They worked 10 hours each day, six days each week. The work was hazardous. The boys were forced to work without gloves to handle the slick coal better. The slate, however, was sharp, and boys would leave work with their fingers cut and bleeding. Many lost fingers to the rapidly

The tall building in the photo is a coal breaker. It's not the Lackawanna but it was also located in Carbondale

moving conveyor belts, while others, moving about the plant, had their feet, hands, arms, and legs amputated when they moved among the machinery and accidentally slipped under the belts or into the gears. Many died when they fell into the gears of the machinery, their bodies not retrieved until the end of the working day. Others were caught in the rush of coal and crushed to death or smothered. The coal created so much dust that the boys sometimes wore lamps on their heads to see, and asthma and black lung disease became common, leading to early deaths.

But the boys in the Lackawanna breaker in 1872 didn't live long enough to die of black lung disease.

The breaker was located about 200 feet from the mouth of a slope that ran into the mine. A track for coal cars ran into the mine along this slope, making a gradual descent. A huge wooden trestle was between the mine and the breaker with a narrow railway laid on top. Cars crossed the trestle and were emptied into the breaker. In addition to the boys who sorted the coal, about 15 other men worked on the trestle and in the breaker. As one newspaper noted in the wake of the disaster, "It was considered safe and was, to all appearances, substantially built."

On the afternoon of April 2, a storm that had been blowing in the region for two days increased its ferocity, and a gust of wind lifted the entire structure of the breaker from its foundation and knocked it over into a deep chasm, taking with it the trestle and the upper portion of the building. As it collapsed, falling more than 100 feet, there was a loud crash - so loud that the people in surrounding towns heard it distinctly.

Hundreds of people flocked to the scene of the disaster, just in time to see the wreckage burst into flames. Miners and volunteers pushed their way through the morbidly curious to try and rescue anyone who might be alive. A reporter on the scene wrote, "Their cries were heartrending, and the scene at this moment among the friends and relatives of the unfortunate victims was indescribable. The air was filled with their groans and wailings."

The first victim found was a little boy named Henry Palmer, who was horribly mangled and dead. Another boy, Thomas Fagan, was taken out next. He was terribly burned, and his skull had been crushed in the fall. Four more boys followed - Dwight Morse, John Clark, William Palmer, and Henry Jones - all badly hurt but not dead. They would all later die in the hospital. Unbelievably, 16 of the men who had also been working in the building had survived, more frightened than hurt.

Those who believed that the woman in black was some sort of "death omen" were convinced the community had been warned of tragedy again.

And then came the sightings in February 1892.

The woman in black was active once again, sending a tremor of fear through the hearts of the local immigrant community. They were terrified that something horrible was going to happen again, just as it did when the woman had been seen before.

And they were right.

On April 20, 1892 - just two months after the woman was seen again - a disaster occurred near the small town of Pottsville, less than an hour from Carbondale. A mine operated by the Lytle Coal Company was flooded when an unknown water source broke through the walls and surged into the mine itself.

The accident occurred when the shifts were changing. Which, at first, made it impossible to know who was in the mine and who had gotten out or had not yet reported to work. The death toll rose by the hour, eventually settling at 12 male American workers. A reply to a reporter from the mine's main office noted there were also many Italian and Hungarian workers in the mine, and it was believed that at least six of them had also drowned.

The company, owned by officials from the Pennsylvania Railroad, had recently re-opened the mine. It had been sitting idle for about two years due to the large water accumulation. Gangways had to be built over surface water areas so that the men could get to the mine entrance. They soon found that working a mine surrounded on all sides with water was a perilous plan.

Those in Carbondale who saw the eerie woman in black walking down the town's streets could have told them that.

There are no other records of the "death omen" of the northeast Pennsylvania coal fields. Whoever this woman was in life, she seems to have fulfilled whatever purpose had been asked of her in death.

As far as I know, she never walked again.

ALMA, NEBRASKA – 1902

The specter of a woman in black made its first known appearance early March 1902, when she was spotted by H.S. Weatherald, the editor of the local newspaper.

He was sitting in his office working one evening on a warm spring night. He had opened the window a few inches and was enjoying the balmy air. Then, without warning, the kerosene lamp on his desk suddenly went out. He assumed that it was a gust of air from the open window, but when he looked over, he saw a woman in a black dress peering through the glass at him. She had a narrow face and piercing eyes and was looking directly at him.

Although startled, he assumed it must be one of his subscribers, so he reached over and raised the window to speak with her - and she vanished.

Weatherald assumed it had been a trick of the eye or a reflection in the glass and tried not to think anymore about it, but then, a few nights later, he was leaving his office and a woman rushed by him, apparently in a great hurry. She was also wearing a black dress - and she also disappeared, no more than 25 feet past him on the sidewalk.

Knowing people would think he had lost his mind, he said nothing of the two strange encounters with the woman and would likely have never told anyone about it if she had not been encountered by someone else a short time later.

Congressman Ashton Shallenberger, who represented the area in the U.S. Congress, was home for a short time from Washington to take care of some private business. The congressman and the newspaper editor were old friends and

Alma, Nebraska in the early 1900s

arranged a dinner one evening. While enjoying after-dinner cigars, Shallenberger made some cautious inquiries about a mysterious woman in black who had been seen in town.

The two men then mutually confessed their encounters to each other.

The congressman was leaving the bank one evening around 10:00 p.m. and had started walking home. As he passed the first alley along his route, he felt a sudden rush of air. A moment later, a woman in a black dress and heavy veil hurried out of the alley in front of him. She walked about 10 feet and then completely vanished. He told the editor the street was dimly lit, but he knew what he had seen.

Within a week, the woman in black had been seen by a dozen different men - and no women. Those who encountered her came from every walk of life and included everyone from leading citizens like carriage dealer Frank Grigsby to Methodist church deacon Wiley Schultz. He had scoffed at the existence of the ghost - until he was pursued by her while walking home one evening.

Days passed with more sightings, and plans began to be made to catch the woman and, if she was a ghost, to put her to rest. But not everyone believed she came from the spirit world. A rumor spread in Alma that the ghost was, in fact, the very alive second wife of an unnamed man in the community.

The man had promised his wife on her deathbed that he would never marry again. She allegedly told him that she would haunt him if he did. He forgot the promise and warning and had married again 18 months after her death. However, his second marriage was not a happy one, and some of the people in Alma believed that the second wife was trying to get even with him by living up to the threat of wife number one. But suspicions ended after the dreaded woman in black was seen by reliable witnesses while the second wife was safely at home.

The mystery of Alma's woman in black was never solved. Many tried to catch her, but she always vanished whenever someone got within 20 feet of her. She continued to rush out at lone male pedestrians throughout the month of March 1902, but then she vanished one night and was never seen again.

Her identity - and the reason for her appearance - has never been explained.

MAHANOY CITY, PENNSYLVANIA - 1903

I could only find one mention of the heavily veiled woman in black who prowled parts of this city for more than a week in February 1903. She appeared each night, pursuing men, women, and children along the dark streets. More than a dozen people claimed the figure had followed them, and all described her as a tall, angular woman.

Several of them claimed the woman also spoke aloud, always admonishing them to "prepare for death."

BRADLEY PARK, NEW JERSEY - 1905

Most of the "death omens" that I have passed along to you in this chapter have been ominous figures in black who appear over and over again, warning the living of calamitous events that are going to occur.

But this story is a little different. Not only did I find the initial story of the "black ghost" by accident, what happened next came as an even bigger surprise. This "portent of doom" only appeared one time, but I think you'll find this account as intriguing as I did.

In early January 1905, reports began trickling in from residents of Bradley Park about a "black ghost" that was seen floating in the air along Bordentown Avenue at night. Two men driving in the country saw it first and described it as a woman in black, wearing a flowing dress and heavy veil. She seemed to glide from the edge of a gravel pit to the center of the road, where she disappeared.

The two men - along with everyone else who reported the ghost over the next few days - all made sure to note the nearest landmark to the sighting.

They all saw it just outside the small, two-room house of a man named Charles Rose.

Two weeks after the first report of the woman in black, on January 25, the West Grove church bell started ringing in the early morning hours, alerting the volunteer firefighters in the community that a blaze had broken out. The alarm had been raised by Clarence McChestney, who lived along Bordentown Avenue, and who spotted a nearby residence in flames.

The home belonged to Charlie Rose.

Unfortunately for Charlie, a snowstorm had moved into the area the night before, and it was later said that most of the firemen did not hear the bells because of the high winds blowing that morning. Only two men - Grant Lott and Ludlow Smith -

made it to the engine house that morning, although the snow was coming down so hard that they didn't recognize each other until they spoke. They waited several minutes for other firefighters to arrive, all the while noting the growing glow of the fire in the distance. When no other company members appeared, they figured that two firemen without apparatus were better than no one at all and trudged away through the snow.

They arrived just in time to pull down the front porch on the house and rob the fire of most of its remaining fuel. The house was soon a smoldering ruin, but the blaze had gone out.

Was the fire just a coincidence? Or was the woman in black trying to warn Charlie - who perished in the fire - that calamity was coming? We'll never know for sure, but you must admit the timing of the ghost sightings and the fire that followed are more than a little strange.

EAST ALTON, ILLINOIS – 1912-1929

The story of the "Olin Woman in Black" has been a part of the Alton, Illinois, folklore for decades now. It's a story that many dismiss as just another legend about a "death omen." But, for many years, workers at the black powder manufacturing company outside of town took it very seriously - so seriously that many of the workers vowed to "shoot the woman on sight" if they ever spotted her.

Her first appearance came in 1917, just before an explosion occurred at the factory, but her origin may date to about five years before. Regardless, every time she appeared outside the plant, walking along Powder Mill Road, it was said that disaster would soon follow.

For as long as this story has been around, people have been asking if it's true. Is it? I'll present the evidence, and you can decide for yourself.

The Equitable Powder Manufacturing Company was started in East Alton in 1892. Its founder, Franklin W. Olin, started the company to provide black powder for blasting in the coal mines of Southern Illinois, but, eventually, the Olin Corporation would become one of the country's greatest producers of sporting guns and ammunition.

The Equitable Powder Manufacturing Company expanded to become the Western Cartridge Company in 1892

It still exists today and is in the same location as Franklin's original factory along Powder Mill Road. It saw its first major growth around the turn of the last century when the company added to its black powder line by producing shotgun ammunition. In 1898, the company expanded with the Western Cartridge Company, an assembly plant using parts from other manufacturers. Soon, competition forced Western Cartridge to start making its own components, and by 1907, it was one of America's top makers of hunting cartridges and ammo. In 1916, a brass mill was added to the operations.

During World War I, Western supplied ammunition to the United States Army as well as to our foreign allies. They were the only commercial company allowed to retain their own primer specifications for their ammunition.

John Olin had joined his father in the firm in 1913. He began making additional changes that would benefit the company, including developing smokeless and progressive burning powders that are still used today. He also led the way to another major step in 1931, when he purchased the famed Winchester Repeating Arms Company of New Haven, Connecticut. This led to the company's development of the M-1 Carbine during World War II.

In the decades that have followed, the Olin Corporation had continued to produce arms and ammunition, tools, and countless other items.

It has also become a part of the legend and lore of the region with the story of the "Woman in Black."

She was first seen in March 1917. America was still embroiled in World War I, and there was little time for ghost stories for the workers at the powder factory. Even so, when stories began to be told about a sinister-looking woman in a black dress and veil who was seen walking along Powder Mill Road, people listened.

Those who saw her described her as completely clothed in black, from her black dress to her hat to the waist-length veil that she wore that obscured her features. Sightings usually occurred after dark, when the night shift was reporting to the plant, but some claimed to see her in the daytime, too. A few tried to approach her, but she promptly vanished when they did. Others said they saw her dart out into the road, caught in the headlights on their automobiles, but she vanished when the vehicles came too close to her.

No one knew who she was, but even the skeptical admitted that it was a harmless distraction from the hard work of the assembly line.

And then there was the explosion.

No one put the accident and the sightings of the woman in black together - not at first - but it would later be said that the timing was unnerving.

On March 8, 1917, Ross Hauveisburk, 21, was killed when a half-million primers exploded. The young man's job was to get the primers from the women in the inspection department and carry them into the vacuum room, where they were put into a large boiler to dry. Once dry, Ross placed them in sacks, where the machines could use them. The primers were extremely volatile, and it was assumed that one of them went off, causing all of them to explode. The vacuum room, a wooden building attached to the main factory, was utterly destroyed. Ross was working alone at the time, so no one else was hurt.

The young man was, of course, not so lucky. The explosion tore him to pieces. Thousands of the little caps from the primers ripped into his body. He was so mutilated that employees who ran to the scene were not allowed to see his corpse.

A coroner's inquest was held the following day but with the only witness - a plant foreman - unable to testify. No one was able to say how the accident had happened.

Ross died, leaving his mother and father and a grieving fiancée behind. He was buried in Bunker Hill, Illinois, where he had grown up.

In February 1919, word spread that the woman in black had been seen again on Powder Mill Road. Several plant employees claimed she had been walking along the side of the road at night. One even claimed that she turned to look at him when he passed her in his car and that her eyes were "shining," even though the rest of her face was obscured by her veil.

On February 26, a man named Tom Collins was severely burned by an explosion at the plant. He was running a black powder machine, and a shell turned upside down and exploded. His clothing caught fire, and before the flames could be put out, his arms, legs, and face were severely burned. He died at the hospital a few days later.

It didn't take much for some of the more superstitious workers at the factory to connect the sightings of the woman in black and the two accidents that had occurred soon after she had been seen.

Rumors quickly spread, and the woman's legend began to grow. More and more people claimed they had seen her before the two accidents, and they embellished the stories by saying that she had spoken to them, warning them of "danger." Others swore that when they had seen her, she was surrounded by a "cold wind."

What was true and what was fiction is impossible to say, but nearly everyone had some theory about who she was and why she appeared along Powder Mill Road. Some claimed that she was merely a "banshee-like death omen," but the more popular theory was that she was a ghost, bringing with her a warning from the spirit world. Others said that she was a living person with uncanny powers - perhaps the widow of someone who had also died at the plant, perhaps in its early days.

Or could she be both of those things?

On October 14, 1912, a young man named Theodore Wilkening died from injuries he sustained in an explosion at the plant. He was working in the loading department of the Western Cartridge Works at a machine that loaded shells. Above him was the "hopper," into which the proper mixture of powder for the shells was placed. Wilkening released the powder mixture by pulling on a cord, and it ran down a pipe to the shells. It was something he did hundreds of times each day without anything out of the ordinary happening - until that day.

As he reached up and pulled the cord to load the next shells, an unexplainable explosion occurred. Wilkening was burned by the 100 pounds of powder in the hopper that had detonated, but the burns weren't what killed him.

The heavy door that was supposed to protect the machine operator flew off. Wilkening turned to try and shield himself, and the door struck him in the right side, breaking a rib. The bone then pierced his right lung, which caused his death at the hospital a short time later.

The 12 other men in the room with him were badly shaken up by the explosion but were not injured.

Workers at the Western Cartridge Company plant.

Only one man died — Theodore Wilkening.

According to the paper, the explosion was plainly felt in nearby East Alton, rattling dishes and shaking windows, but that was nothing compared to the pain suffered by Theodore's wife, who was paralyzed by grief by her young husband's death. A short time later, she also died, unable to eat or sleep in the wake of the accident.

Or so the story goes.

Many came to believe that the woman in black was Theodore's wife, still in her mourning dress, trying to warn others of impending death at the factory.

If it truly was her, then it explains why the sightings of the woman in black began again in the summer of 1923.

Just a few weeks after the woman in black returned to her grim stroll along Powder Mill Road, another deadly accident occurred at the Western Cartridge Company, this time taking the lives of more than a dozen people, including seven women.

On July 10, 1923, an explosion occurred inside one of six machines taking apart cartridges salvaged from the U.S. Army after the war ended. Nearly 50 men and women worked at the six machines, feeding in the cartridges. The machines removed the bullets, emptied the powder, removed the caps, and reclaimed every part of the shell, separating them to go to different parts of the factory. Powder was scattered everywhere, but special precautions had been taken to guard against accidents.

But those precautions were not quite good enough.

Suddenly, there was a flash of one of the powder cans, and fire sparked from the machine. There was a loud blast, and flying metal pieces went in every direction. Everyone around the machines was injured in some way, but five of the workers - William Brummer, Anna Gorman, Frank Bennes, Howard Hunter, and Hazel Young - were killed instantly. About 18 others were severely injured, and seven more died at the hospital before the day was over.

The explosion broke every window in the room, but the resulting fire did little damage to the brick and metal structure. If only the living had fared so well. The skulls of several of the dead had been crushed like tissue paper from flying metal and wood. Bones were broken, limbs severed, and ghastly wounds were inflicted on their bodies.

Ambulances and firefighters raced to the scene, and survivors were taken to nearby hospitals. A few who escaped with little injury were treated at the scene.

When news of the explosion spread, a crowd gathered at the factory's gates, made up mainly of the family members and friends of those killed or hurt. As word was brought out about some maimed worker or a dead body, the atmosphere grew tense until that person's identity was learned. Some member of the group was sure to collapse when news arrived. Women with their faces buried in their hands, sobbing, were led away by kind friends. Mothers and families anxiously waited for news of a son or husband and would break down and sob in relief upon hearing he was safe.

Ambulances would come clanging back to the gate from the factory, and as each of them came out, the crowd surged forward to see who was inside. Many fought their way to the front of the group to be either happy or heartbroken. It was a pitiful scene. Women wept, and men broke down into tears.

But all the while, there were the little groups that whispered among themselves. They murmured about both the living and the dead, but there were those among them who whispered of someone else - the woman in black.

When gossip began to spread throughout the factory that the woman in black had been seen again the year after the terrible explosion, many were angrier than they were afraid. Some went as far as to say that if they saw the woman on Powder Mill Road, she would be "shot on sight." She was no longer regarded as a benevolent spirit offering a warning but as a bad luck omen of doom.

But that didn't prevent the sightings from taking place. In late June and early July 1924, the woman was back at her task, prowling the edge of the road and being spotted by mill employees on their way to work.

A disaster seemed inevitable.

Despite the care that was taken to prevent another accident, one happened anyway - exactly one year to the day of the 1923 explosion.

On July 10, Leslie Cunningham was badly injured in a blast that ripped apart the building where he was working. The 30-year-old operator was in charge of the blending plant and was luckily working alone. Because there were no witnesses, the cause of the explosion remains a mystery. However, investigators at the time surmised that a small flame could have set off the ton of smokeless powder in the blending room.

Although in the plant alone, Cunningham was not the only worker injured. Iva Herron was the driver of a horse team that hauled and made deliveries around the plant. With him on the wagon was his assistant, A.J. Rice. They were passing by the blending mill when the explosion occurred, and both men were injured.

Ambulances rushed them to St. Joseph's Hospital, where all three were treated. Herron and Rice, who were about 35 yards from the building when the explosion took place, were treated for burns, but Cunningham was not as lucky. He died in the hospital the following day. He never regained consciousness.

The woman in black, it was said, had predicted disaster once again.

And she was not quite finished.

As far as I can discover, the woman appeared one more time on Powder Mill Road in the winter of 1929. She made several appearances to workers as they neared the factory and then disappeared as mysteriously as she had every time over the last two decades.

On February 19, Roy Fallin was killed in an explosion at the plant. He was working alone at the time, and because of that, the cause of the accident will never be known. Officials believed, though, that he may have dropped a rubber cup containing a priming mixture - or he stumbled and fell - causing the mixture to explode.

Fallin, a Pentecostal minister, was employed as a carrier of the priming mixture about 30 yards from a storehouse to the building where primers were made. The fact that this was his sole job gives us an idea of just how dangerous it was.

The mixture had to be struck, or there must be a concussion for it to explode. Whether it was dropped or Fallin tripped, some force was apparently applied to it, causing it to detonate. Since he was outside when it happened, no one else was hurt.

It turned out to be fatal for Roy, though., The force of the blast fractured his legs and lacerated his hip and one hand. He died in the hospital six hours later, likely from shock.

The woman in black was never seen again after Fallin's death. It wasn't as though she had caused it - if we decide that she was real - but she had predicted it, just as she had so many others.

Why did her appearances stop after that? No one knows. Perhaps she had simply served her time, or possibly improving safety standards in the industry just didn't make her warnings as important as they once were.

After 1929, the woman in black left Powder Mill Road and firmly entrenched herself in the legend and lore of America's sinister strangers.

FROM SLENDERMAN TO THE SHADOW PEOPLE

MODERN VERSIONS OF THE "BLACK GHOST"

The "Black Ghosts" of the late nineteenth and early twentieth century were the urban legends of their time. Leaving aside the possibly legitimate sightings for a moment, there is no question that many of the encounters with black ghosts can be written off to rumor, gossip, and wild imagination. As anxiety gripped the towns where such figures were reported, it's natural to assume that some of the reports were based on what people imagined they saw. As more and more stories piled up, officials were baffled by their inability to catch what people were claiming to see, let alone track down solid evidence of their existence. Legends were then born, largely based on what might not have necessarily been the truth.

Before we go any further down that path, I need to say that I am not implying that *none* of the encounters were real. *Something* was happening across America. There was no 24-hour news cycle at the time, no internet, no text messaging, no social media. And yet, somehow, people had remarkably similar encounters with the unknown in the form of threatening figures in black.

I do think *something* was out there, but I also feel that often in the communities where encounters were happening, legends grew based on fiction, not fact. Kind of like a turn of the last century version of *Creepypasta*, the internet-age collection of frightening and imaginary characters of horror, legend, and the macabre that is sometimes mistaken for real life. When that happens, *Creepypasta* figures become sort of the "black ghosts" of the modern-day.

Creepypasta was born from the internet slang term *copypasta*, which in turn came from the old "copy and paste" command that first made it easy to share information and creative efforts online. Contributors to *Creepypasta* share their tales to be shocking and collaborate with others to create never-ending stories, often using figures and characters that are believed to be real by many readers - characters like the Wendigo, Goat Man, Michigan Dogman, and others.

Sharing these stories can even make *Creepypasta* characters "come to life," especially when it deals with figures that many believe are already real, albeit anomalous, characters, like the ones mentioned above - or worse.

In May 2014, two girls from Waukesha, Wisconsin, became obsessed with a popular *Creepypasta* figure called "Slenderman," a tall, inhumanly thin figure with a blank face and a penchant for wearing evening clothes. The girls came to believe that he would invite them to live with him in the forest if they killed someone to prove their devotion to him. They knew, according to his mythology, that Slenderman was linked to missing children in towns across the Midwest - fictional children and fictional towns, by the way.

They ended up stabbing a friend 19 times and leaving her for dead. But she survived the attack to tell the authorities what happened, and the two girls were charged with attempted murder.

But Slenderman was never real. He was a fiction that influenced a very real-life crime. He was no more real than the other modern legends that have been created in the eras of the internet, like the "Hat Man," another character created out of thin air that likely has more to do with sleep paralysis than the paranormal.

The Hat Man was born on Twitter, the social media site, when numerous people began making claims of waking up in the dark to find a shadowy figure in a hat looming over them. The encounters have attracted a lot of attention, inspiring documentaries, and a blog where people can share their experiences.

But it turns out that the Hat Man is not a new phenomenon. For as long as written records have existed, people have described a frightening night-time vision that paralyzes them with fear and seems to suck the life out of them. In the Middle Ages, it was caused by demons. Native Americans believed it was a witch. The Japanese blamed a ghost. Modern science, though, calls it "sleep paralysis," when an individual, in the process of falling asleep or awakening, finds themselves completely awake but unable to move or speak. Frequently, they see a shadowy or indistinct shape standing over them and become increasingly terrified.

Sleep paralysis is a common occurrence, affecting many on a regular basis. Just why or how it happens isn't clear. Researchers believe sleep paralysis is caused by a disturbed rapid eye movement cycle because it mostly happens as people fall into or come out of REM sleep. During that stage, their brains normally paralyze their muscles anyway -- so they don't act out their dreams. But during sleep paralysis, the sleeper is awake or half-awake and is aware they cannot move.

Studies show that between 25% and 50% of Americans have had sleep paralysis at least once. Sleep experts believe sleep paralysis might be partly genetic. Other causes include stress and disrupted sleep schedules, caused by travel or perhaps staying up all night to study. Several studies have also found links between social anxiety or panic disorder and sleep paralysis.

Clearly, an episode of sleep paralysis can be scary. Often the experience is accompanied by noises, sensations of being dragged out of bed or flying, and difficulty breathing. In fact, some researchers believe sleep paralysis might be the cause behind accounts of alien abduction.

And then there are the figures like the Hat Man, a dark, black shape with no features, only a silhouette with a wide-brimmed hat. What sleepers are seeing is very real to them, and they react to an image that seems to be very similar across individuals, cultures, and different parts of the world - helped along by the internet.

But why a man in a hat? Some experts say the idea of the Hat Man may be subconscious reworkings of figures from popular culture, including popular horror characters from the movies - like Freddy Krueger. The villain from *A Nightmare on Elm Street* not only attacks people in their sleep but also wears the exact kind of hat that the Hat Man reportedly wears.

And then there are the "Shadow People," another type of menacing figure that has gained popularity in recent times, even though its origins are said to be much older.

There have been descriptions of shadowy, human-like shapes - like Black Ghosts - in folklore and religious texts throughout history. They include the ancient Islamic beings known as Djinn and the shadowy beings known as the *Nalusa Chito* of the Choctaw nation. The modern version of these creatures, known simply as "Shadow People," are said to be phantom forms often observed standing at the end of a hallway, in a dark bedroom, or in our peripheral vision.

In other words, in places where the sightings can never really be verified.

Fear of the dark is a common phobia, probably because our eyes play tricks on us when the lights are low. A jacket hanging on a door can easily become the silhouette of a man, and a pile of blankets can suddenly look like someone lurking in your bed.

But proponents of the reality of Shadow People will try to convince you there is more to them than that.

It seems that no one in the paranormal community can agree about what Shadow People are - or even if they exist. Some believe they are ghosts or bundles of negative energy, while others go way out on a limb and claim they are evil, malicious beings that can be vanquished by rebuking them in the name of Jesus. One thing that believers in the phenomenon can agree on, though, is that they are unsettling, no matter their origin. Most who report seeing them say they feel an overwhelming dread, terror, and in some cases as if paralyzed with fear.

Skeptics have more straightforward explanations than malicious demons. They chalk most Shadow People sightings up to sleep paralysis - much like the Hat Man - heightened emotional states, sleep deprivation, or substance abuse.

It's also important to note that most sightings of Shadow People occur in very murky light or in our peripheral vision, which is designed to detect motion and movement, not detail. That said, it would be easier to mistake something in the corner of our eye for something it isn't than it would be if we were to see something head-on.

Does that explain every encounter? Of course not - no more than saying that "hysteria" can explain every sighting of a Black Ghost in the early 1900s. My plan here was not to dispel the notion that such figures might exist but instead to draw the comparison between our culture then and our culture now when it comes to the dark things that go bump in the night.

2. AMERICA AND "SPRING-HEELED JACK"

In 1838, a strange figure literally leapt into the public's imaginations. He sprang over walls and hedges from dark alleyways and grim graveyards to frighten and physically attack women.

He appeared first in the twilight world of Victorian London, eventually making his way to smaller towns that were not served by the new railways - to places where gas and electricity had not been installed and a world where news took time to get from place to place.

The newspaper reports of a mysterious leaping man created a national hysteria response, and they led to copycat attacks, even wilder stories, and extraordinary claims of the sinister stranger's real identity, fueling the paranoia that was already running rampant across England.

People who claimed to see the figure who became known as "Spring-Heeled Jack" described him as having a terrifying appearance, with bat-like wings, clawed hands, and eyes that resembled circles of fire. Some reports claimed that, under his

black cloak, he wore a huge helmet and a tight-fitting oilskin garment. Others said he was tall and thin, with the appearance of a gentleman. Several accounts even claimed that he breathed blue flames.

In recent times, some researchers have attempted to suggest who he might have been - including an alien visitor from another planet - but none of these theories really hold water.

Jack remains an enigma and a larger-than-life character that influenced many aspects of Victorian life, especially in London. His name was conjured up as a "bogeyman," scaring children into behaving by telling them that if they weren't good, Jack would get them.

But in a book about America's sinister strangers, how does the very British figure of Spring-Heeled Jack fit into the mix? Well, it seems that Jack - or at least some version of him - has made many appearances here, too.

THE ORIGINAL SPRING-HEELED JACK

The sightings began in late 1837, when Jack started prowling the lanes of Middlesex, scaring - and sometimes tearing - the pants off the locals. The press wouldn't take notice of his antics for a few months yet, amidst allegations that they had been paid to ignore the story.

A first report appeared in the London Times on January 9, 1838, concerning sightings in Peckham, a small village south of London. In the days that followed, the authorities were deluged with reports of a tall, thin intruder with a prominent nose and bony fingers that resembled claws. He was incredibly agile and wore a long, flowing cloak that billowed behind him as he leapt over walls, hedges, and fences. He wore a tall, metallic helmet on his head, and under his cloak were close-fitting garments of some shiny material, perhaps oilskin. Even odder, he seemed to have some sort of lamp strapped to his chest.

London's Lord Mayor took action and oversaw the formation of a vigilance committee made up of magistrates, former army officers, and others. Police patrols scoured the area where the figure had been seen, and a reward fund was set up in hopes the man could be captured.

But there seemed to be little chance of that. Jack seemed to break every law that should have slowed him down - from legal statutes to the laws of physics. People started calling the creature "Spring-Heeled Jack" because he seemed to have actual springs in his shoes, which allowed him to clear a road in a single bound and leap over eight-foot walls. Jack soared over the heads of his would-be captors, passed over bushes with a single stride, and, on one occasion, leaped over a wagon. He seemed impossible to catch.

Sightings of Jack followed a trail along the river, working upstream to the west before crossing the Thames. Then he traveled from village to village until he reached the grounds of Kensington Palaces, where he stayed for some time. He was reported climbing over the park wall at midnight and dancing on the wooded lawns - or so the stories went.

The sightings created a panic that only got worse with each passing day. Those without escorts stayed inside at night. No one wanted to meet Jack in a dark alley - but soon, he couldn't be avoided.

On February 20, 1838, Jane Alsop, 18, who lived at Bear Bine Cottage, was disturbed by the violent ringing of the front doorbell. She went out and found a person there who seemed to be wearing the hat and cloak of the police horse patrol. It was only when she lit a lamp that she saw the "most hideous appearance" of Spring-Heeled Jack, who pulled aside his cloak to reveal tight, shiny garments and a flashing lamp on his chest.

Jane screamed, and then things went badly wrong. The man seized her arm in the iron grip of his claw-like fingers, tearing at her dress and hair. Jack spurted "blue and white flames" into her face, and Jane lost consciousness. Thankfully, her father and sister came to her rescue, and their testimony, along with Jane's injuries, corroborated the story.

Despite this, the officers that conducted the investigation concluded Jane had been so terrified that she'd mistaken her attacker for Spring-Heeled Jack and dismissed the events.

Eight days later, Lucy Scales was attacked by a man fitting the same description. Lucy had been waiting for her sister, who noted that the man she saw was "tall, thin, and gentlemanly" until he opened his long cape and revealed a flashing light that was attached to his chest. There was no time to scream - Jack's weird blue and white flames struck Lucy in the face, and she dropped to the ground unconscious.

A week later, on February 27, Jack attacked one last time. He knocked on the door of a house on Turner Street, off

Commercial Road. A servant boy opened the door and was confronted by the startling figure on the doorstep. He let out a scream, drawing the attention of neighbors, and Jack fled.

It was the last time that Spring-Heeled Jack appeared in London. After that day, he vanished as if the ground had swallowed him up. The police investigations went cold, and the stories eventually died out. Hoaxers invoked Jack's name from time to time, and for years afterward, nighttime encounters on the roadways revived the legend, but the real Jack was gone.

Or was he?

Now and then, new stories appeared. In the 1860s, two women walking along a road in the moonlight saw a tall figure clad in "some very fantastic garment" soar over a hedge on the side of the road and land a few yards in front of them. It then bounded over a tall fencerow on the other side of the road and was lost to sight.

In 1872, a "ghost," as some witnesses called it, began prowling the Peckham area. It was said to leap over fences and walls that were too high for an ordinary man to scale. In Sheffield, the following year, people reported seeing a tall figure who "sprang like a goat."

In 1877, a figure many believed was Jack merrily bounded from rooftop to rooftop in Norfolk, and nearly every resident in the community witnessed the spectacle.

In August of that same year, sentries on guard at military barracks in Aldershot claimed Jack appeared from nowhere and slapped them. Several claimed they shot the figure, but it apparently had no effect.

A 1904 newspaper report from Liverpool seems to mark Jack's last appearance in England, although weirdly, stories continued to circulate about him well into the 1930s, a century after he first appeared.

So, who was Jack?

No one knows but no matter how bizarre his appearance and behavior, Spring-Heeled Jack was always assumed by the authorities to be a real person.

Rumors spread that Jack may have been the Third Marquis of Waterford, Henry de La Poer Beresford, a young Irish nobleman of sordid reputation. His drunken antics earned him the nickname of "the Mad Marquis." He was known to be such a lover of wild parties that he was the man behind an incident that created the phrase "painting the town red."

Henry lived near the locations of the early 1837 and 1838 attacks, and the sightings of Jack came to an end after he left London and went back to Ireland. He died in 1859.

Henry did have an extravagant and unruly reputation. Today, his stunts would land him in jail or at least splashed all over social media, but they were always tempered with humor and were followed by compensation for any damage that he'd done. Terrorizing the city and attacking young women was a bit out of character for him, no matter how drunk he might be.

And there was still the question of Jack's strange costume, the flashing light on his chest, the white and blue flames, and, especially, his ability to leap over walls and onto rooftops. Unless Henry had hired someone to put springs into his boots, it seems unlikely that he was the sinister boogeyman that prowled the city streets and alleys.

No other suspects have ever been seriously considered, largely because Jack seemed to have no real purpose or motive. The authorities referred to Jack's appearances as "pranks," and newspapers pointed out that "certain it is that robbery was not the motive, for he was never known to take a single coin from his victims."

Despite Jack's physical attacks on his victims, his intention seemed to be scaring them, not killing them - just like the sinister strangers that appear in almost every chapter of this book.

And like those other figures, he was there one day and then gone the next, vanished without a trace. In the case of Spring-Heeled Jack, though, that doesn't seem to be the end of the story.

LEAPING ACROSS THE WATER

The legend of Spring-Heeled Jack didn't end in 1904 - and, in fact, didn't even come to an end in England. Jack - or at least figures that sound a lot like him - began showing up in America in the twentieth century.

In the summer of 1938, four children in Silver City, New Mexico, claimed to see a man in gray, close-fitting clothing fly over them at treetop height. One of the witnesses, Ann Alley, reported that "he seemed to be wearing a belt which was wide and had points sticking out of it. He also seemed to be wearing a cap."

In the fall of that same year, residents in Provincetown, Massachusetts, an isolated community on the very tip of Cape Cod, began reporting a mysterious attacker that was alleged to be nearly seven feet tall. He was always described the same way - gigantic, fast, and ugly. He was always dressed in a black hood and cape that flapped behind him like hideous bat wings. He had fierce-looking eyes and pointed ears, breathed blue fire into his victim's faces, and, most importantly, he vaulted over fences and walls that were at least eight feet high.

The sightings started around Halloween 1938, the off-season for the tourist area when the streets and beaches were empty and quiet. It was the children who saw it first - a sinister-looking black shape among the dunes or down dark allies. The adults wrote it off as a prank until they started to see it, too.

A woman named Maria Costa came face-to-face with the figure on Commercial Street, near the Town Hall. As she started to cross the road to a coffee shop, she saw a figure moving in the shadows. Suddenly, it jumped right at her as if it were on springs, the black cape spreading

Commercial Street in Provincetown in the 1930s

lout like wings. Maria froze, too terrified to even scream. It loomed over her for a moment - close enough to touch her - and then it was gone. Maria later told the police, "He was black, all black with eyes like balls of flame. And he was big, maybe eight-feet-tall." Most unsettling, she said the figure made a buzzing sound, like a huge insect.

Over the next few weeks, dozens of people saw the figure. He - or it - had a habit of leaping out at people from behind trees and houses or dropping down on them from a rooftop. In one case, a man chased what locals were calling the "Phantom of Provincetown" but was quickly outdistanced by what seemed to be superhuman speed on the part of the mysterious figure.

Reluctantly, the Provincetown police began to realize that the bizarre reports that had been coming in were true, but they weren't sure what to do about it. The Phantom had not broken any laws or harmed anyone or their property - but that was soon to change.

However, not before things took a strange turn. One night, a terrified boy burst into the police station after a close encounter with the Phantom. "It jumped out at me from nowhere," the shaken young man cried, "and spit blue flames into my face!"

A dog that belonged to local resident Charles Farley cornered the stranger in the yard. Farley hurried outside with a shotgun in his hands to find a tall, black monster with what he swore was long, silver ears. "I thought it was some kind of animal," Farley said, "So, I shot it."

But the shotgun blast seemed to have no effect on it. Farley claimed that "the darn thing just laughed and jumped my eight-foot-high fence in one leap."

Reports flooded the police department phone lines, with callers claiming to see the figure on opposite sides of town within minutes of each other. They were sure that something supernatural was in their midst.

But the police were not convinced of that. Along with the most skeptical residents, the authorities were putting together a list of human suspects. But none of the investigations went anywhere. As a few years passed and some of the suspects went off to fight in World War II, the Phantom remained in Provincetown.

In the early 1940s, fisherman George Loboas encountered the figure on the town common. George was a burly man, known for his great strength and reputation as a brawler, so he wasn't frightened when the black shape jumped out at him. George took a swing at the Phantom, but the figure grabbed his fist and squeezed it so hard that it brought the fisherman to his knees.

George wasn't the only one to fall victim to the intruder. A local pool shark, known as "Eightball Charlie," ran into the Phantom on his way home one dark and chilly fall night. As he was climbing a hill near his house, a huge black shape slid across the street in front of him. He later said he could see glowing eyes under the figure's hood.

Unwilling to run or back down, Charlie called, "You better get out of my way, or I'll smack you one!"

Before Charlie could react, the figure rushed at him and slapped him so hard across the face that it knocked him down. Charlie, somehow, got to his feet and ran home.

The confrontations continued, and the figure was seen by men, women, and children alike. Violent encounters were rare, but they did happen. The entire town remained at a low level of hysteria throughout every fall and winter. It seemed that once the tourists went home, the Phantom returned to take their place.

On a cold night in November 1945, a series of telephone calls came into police headquarters reporting that the Phantom was skulking about the grounds of the Bradford School.

Thinking this might be a real break in the case, Sergeant Francis Marshall rushed to the scene. He knew the grounds of the school well. They were fenced, and there was only one way in or out. If he and his other officers were quick, they might be able to trap the Phantom.

With their headlights and sirens off, two police cars sped to the entrance of the schoolyard. One officer stayed outside the fence while three others - armed with pistols and flashlights - converged at the entrance. They entered the shadowy yard, one by one.

"I've got him!" one of the men yelled.

The Phantom was against the fence, seemingly trapped by the four men who were moving toward him. Sergeant Marshall got his first - and only - look at the figure. Later, he would say that the terrifying silver face must have been some sort of mask. But it was big - as big as the witnesses claimed that it was.

The figure was warned not to move, and it just laughed. It turned its back on the officer and, with a single leap, vaulted into the air and over the 10-foot fence that surrounded the schoolyard. A moment later, it was gone.

There were more sightings of the Phantom after that, but the last incident occurred a few weeks later on a foggy December afternoon. The four Janard children - Al, Joey, Elanore, and Louie -- were playing outside at their home on Standish when Elanore told the others that there was a bear on a sandy hill nearby. They looked and saw, barely visible through the fog, a black figure crawling down the hill toward them.

It wasn't a bear, they realized; it was the Phantom.

With their parents away from the house, they knew they had to defend themselves. They ran into the house and grabbed knives, rolling pins, and a baseball bat. They had locked the front door but were terrified when they saw the doorknob start to turn back and forth. The door shook on its frame, and the children quickly hid. They were sure it would be inside the house with them at any moment.

But the Phantom didn't come inside. It continued to rattle the doorknob and make heavy breathing sounds, but it didn't try to force the door open.

Meanwhile, Louie had grabbed a bucket, filled it with hot water, and tiptoed upstairs to a window over the front door. He leaned out and could see the black figure below - and he dumped the hot water on it.

The children downstairs heard a splash, followed by a startled cry, and that was all. The Phantom fled the scene.

As far as I can find, the mysterious figure was never seen again. What was it? No one can say. Though the incidents were widely reported in the area, no one thought to link it to the century-old story of Spring-Heeled Jack. It was little-known in the United States at the time.

On June 18, 1953, three residents of Houston, Texas, were sitting outside to escape the heat around 2:30 a.m. and spotted a "huge shadow" crossing the lawn in front of them. They saw it "bounce upward into a pecan tree." A pale gray light illuminated a figure in the tree - a tall man with a "black cape, skin-tight pants, and quarter-length boots." He was dressed in "gray or black tight-fitting clothes." One witness thought she saw wings on the figure, but this was likely an illusion caused by the cape. After a few minutes, the figure vanished.

Police officers who investigated the incident judged the witnesses to be sincere and genuinely frightened. Again, neither the witnesses nor the police thought to connect the figure who bounced into the tree with Spring-Heeled Jack.

A few years later, occult writer John A. Keel interviewed an Ohio farm woman and her son who told him a strange story. In 1963 or 1964, mysterious figures had killed some of their cattle but, strangely, had only taken inedible parts of the animals like eyes, brains, and udders. But even stranger, they had gotten a look at the men and described them as tall, wearing close-fitting overalls, and able to "leap over high fences from a standing start."

These incidents were certainly odd, but none of them conjured up the connections to the original Spring-Heeled Jack like the figure in Baltimore in the summer of 1951 did.

THE HORROR IN O'DONNELL HEIGHTS

No one knows when the first sighting occurred or who filed the first report, but there's no doubt that the summer of 1951 was a weird time in Baltimore.

The city sweltered under a heatwave, and only the wealthiest residents could afford air conditioners at the time. There were no air conditioners to be found in O'Donnell Heights, a housing project on the southwest side of the city. This was a place where steel mill and shipyard workers lived with their families.

For those folks, though, the overpowering heat was less of a worry than the specter that was stalking their streets.

At some point in July, a tall, thin figure, dressed all in black, began sprinting across the rooftops of O'Donnell Heights. It leapt on and off buildings, broke into houses, attacked people, enticed a young girl to crawl under a car, and played music in the nearby graveyard. Groups of young men patrolled the streets while others waited by their windows at night, keeping a sleepy watch for the "Phantom Prowler" that eluded his pursuers and vanished into the cemetery before he could be caught. By the end of the month, police were arresting people for disorderly conduct and carrying weapons, but the phantom had disappeared and was never seen again.

What in the hell happened in O'Donnell Heights in the summer of 1951? To this day, no one can say for sure.

O'Donnell Heights was only eight years old when the sinister stranger began making his appearances. Built as a housing project for defense industry workers at Bethlehem Steel, Martin Aircraft, and Edgewood Arsenal during World War II, it was never meant to last long or be pleasing to look at. Tightly-spaced, two-story row houses went up on 66 acres of what used to be farmland, a brickyard that belonged to the Baltimore Brick Company, and part of St. Stanislaus Kostka Cemetery, one of several graveyards in the immediate area. There were other cemeteries nearby, but the phantom soon turned out to have an affinity for St. Stanislaus and usually showed up there.

By the time the local newspapers realized that something very strange was happening in the Heights, the panic was almost over. Most of the stories that remain today come from the back pages of the *Baltimore Sun*, which printed a handful of articles between July 25 and July 27, when the sightings came to an end. Reporters approached it as a "tongue in cheek" story with cartoon illustrations. No one seemed to know when the events had started, but on July 24, Agnes Martin told a reporter that the phantom had been seen for "at least two or three weeks."

The first definite date was July 19, although the figure had undoubtedly been seen several times before. On this day, though, there was a full moon, and nighttime temperatures were in the 70's. It was around 1:00 a.m. when William Buskirk, age 20, ran into the phantom.

He later said: "I was walking along the 1100 block of Travers Way with several buddies when I saw him on a roof. He jumped off the roof, and we chased him into the graveyard...." One of the other boys interviewed with Buskirk stated, "he sure is an athlete. You should have seen him go over that fence - just like a cat." The fence surrounding the cemetery was six feet in height and trimmed with barbed wire around the top. According to the witnesses, the figure in black had leaped over it with ease.

Hazel Jenkins claimed that the phantom grabbed her some time the same week. She saw it twice at close-range and may have been attacked when the figure tried to break into the Jenkins home -- the article isn't clear -- but her brother, Randolph, saw it soon after. He told a reporter: "I saw him two nights after he tried to break into our house... He was just beginning to climb up on the roof of the Community Building. We chased him all the way to Graveyard Hill."

The phantom next visited the family of Melvin Hensler, breaking into their house on July 20 but stealing nothing. After this unnerving experience, the family went to stay with Mr. Hensler's brother, but Mrs. Hensler returned to the house the next day and found "a potato bag left on the ironing board," which she was convinced belonged to the intruder.

Storms on July 23 lowered the temperatures but did not affect the phantom. In fact, on July 24, he was especially active. Newspapers reported: "At 11:30 p.m. officers Robert Clark and Edward Powell were called to the O'Donnell Heights area where they were greeted by some 200 people who said that had seen the oft-reported 'phantom.' Clark said that they pointed to the rooftops, and someone yelled: 'The phantom's there!'" The police drove around and arrested a 23-year-old sailor carrying a hammer. He was fined $5.

A newspaperman reported that he had found 30 or 40 people around the back stoop of a house on Gusryan Street, waiting for the sun to come up. One of them, Charles Pittinger, had armed himself with a shotgun. The newspaperman interviewed several of them, who passed along rumors and told of their own experiences. Some claimed the phantom lived in the graveyard, and a woman who lived on Wellsbach Way, adjacent to St. Stanislaus, suggested that the phantom was doing more than jumping fences and breaking into houses: "One night I heard someone playing the organ in that chapel up there. It was about 1 o'clock."

The phantom was also reportedly seen beckoning to Esther Martin from underneath an automobile, saying, "Come here, little girl."

The consensus of the crowd was that the phantom easily leapt from two-story buildings, flew over fences, and was a general nuisance in the neighborhood. A man named George Cook admitted having mixed feelings about what was happening. He did not deny the reports of the phantom, just the possibility that something extraordinary was involved. In the end, he blamed the media. "It's ridiculous to believe that a man can jump from a height and not leave a mark on the ground. Yet this character does it all the time. It's my idea that when this thing is cleared up... it'll turn out to be one of these young hoodlums who has got the idea from the movies or the so-called funny papers and is trying to act it out. This sort of thing appeals to detective story readers who are mainly looking for excitement."

Meanwhile, the police were busy ignoring the phantom and rounding up the "usual suspects." On the morning of July 25, they arrested four boys on disorderly conduct charges at an unidentified cemetery. Around 10:00 p.m. that same night, officers arrested three boys on an embankment near the cemetery. Their six companions, all on the lookout for the phantom, fled the scene. An hour later, the police responded to a call from a resident who heard footsteps on his roof, but nothing was found. At some point the next day, Mrs. Mildred Gaines heard someone trying to break into her house and ran outside barefoot screaming, "It's the phantom!" It was actually the police breaking down the door to serve a search warrant on the premises. Mrs. Gaines and four male companions were arrested on bookmaking charges.

By this time, the newspaper coverage - which had started with reporters as baffled as the residents of O'Donnell Heights - turned humorous. The stories poked fun at the sightings, reported pranks by neighbors pretending to be the phantom, and carried a story about a phantom sighting on a rooftop that turned out to be a ventilation pipe. On July 27, it was announced there were no more reports and that "Police think it might be a teenager." The phantom was gone, but the heat was back, with high humidity and temperatures in the middle 90's.

Like most of the bizarre events of this type, there was no satisfying resolution to the panic created by the "Phantom of O'Donnell Heights." An unofficial version claimed that residents finally chased it into the cemetery, where the phantom jumped into a crypt and vanished for good.

No one can say who -- or what -- this figure may have been, although based on the sheer number of sightings, something weird was happening in the neighborhood. Descriptions of the phantom were fairly consistent, considering that the encounters were brief, took place in the dark, and he was usually moving at high speed. William Buskirk said, "He was a tall thin man dressed all in black. It looked like he had a cape around him." The only one who mentioned the phantom's face was witness Myrtle Ellen, who said it was horrible. She also agreed about the dark costume. The newspapers described the phantom as "black robed," suggesting long, loose-flowing clothes. Mrs. Melvin Hensler, the discoverer of the discarded potato sack, saw the phantom three times and said that during one sighting, it looked as though he had a hump on his back.

Theories abound about the "Horror of the Heights." Sociologists have described the events in O'Donnell Heights as an example of an "imaginary community threat," suggesting that the 900 families living there experienced some type of mass hysteria whipped up by rumors and the media. It's true that misconceptions undoubtedly played a part in the events, but they don't explain the relatively straightforward experiences described by William Buskirk and other witnesses. The police never denied that people were seeing something but, like George Cook, thought it would turn out to be a "young hoodlum." But if it was, he was never caught, exposed, or forced to confess.

It's also hard to accept that the newspapers played a part in creating any hysteria. The two local papers ran only six articles on the phantom, two of them mere fillers, and they were printed as the sensation was coming to an end. The only one that might be called "sensationalistic" ran on July 25 and included the experiences of several witnesses. However, it ended on a sober note: "The question of the prowler of O'Donnell Heights continued to be not one of the phantoms but of people reacting to (and possibly creating) the unknown with their imaginations."

There were no comparisons made to Spring-Heeled Jack at the time, but it's hard to miss their similarities.

Whatever it was that haunted O'Donnell Heights that summer remains a mystery and one that - like Spring-Heeled Jack himself -- will simply never be solved.

3. AMERICAN VAMPIRES

The city of New Orleans is a place filled with "sinister strangers" of both the supernatural and criminal variety. There are the "Night Doctors" - legendary denizens of the night who operated on poor African Americans and formerly enslaved people; the "Needle Men" - mysterious figures who injected unsuspecting residents with poisons and drugs; and even the "Axeman" - a real-life serial killer who carried out a series of murders in the city around 1918 and claimed to be a "demon sent from hell."

But over the last three decades or so, New Orleans had also become the modern-day capital of another kind of sinister stranger - the vampire. For those who like to dress up like a vampire or even think they are a vampire, this is the right place for them. New Orleans embraces every kind of alternative lifestyle, so vampires are no exception.

Vampire-like creatures have existed in the world's folklore since almost the beginning of recorded history, dating back even to the legends of the

Sumerians, the Babylonians, and the Ancient Egyptians. But a true, traditional vampire was originally a Slavic monster, bringing fear to the superstitious in Eastern Europe -- Hungary, Czechoslovakia, Rumania, the Balkan countries, and their neighbors. Even the word "vampire" is an adaptation of the word *vampir*, which also had close ties to Bulgarian and Russian words that mean the same thing. It is believed that the vampire legend began to grow in notoriety around the sixteenth century. Within the next few decades, a considerable amount of vampire activity began to be reported, creating eerie tales and haunting stories throughout the region. By the 1700s, all of Europe began to be obsessed by these undead creatures who left their coffins at night, drained the blood from the living, and could only be defended against by holy water, crucifixes, and stakes through the heart.

New Orleans vampire lore allegedly began around this same time, when young French girls began arriving at the old Ursuline convent, getting off the boat with the casket-shaped boxes that held all their belongings. They had been brought to the colony as potential wives for the love-starved male settlers who had previously been chasing Choctaw women through the woods, looking for affection. The girls from France were known as *filles a la cassette* or the "casket girls."

Their caskets boxes were stored in the convent's attic on the third floor. When some of those cases were discovered to be empty, rather than think a light-fingered sailor had stolen their possessions, superstitious citizens spread rumors that the casket girls had smuggled vampires into New Orleans.

They hadn't, but a story is a story, I guess.

They then go on to say that the caskets are still stored in the attic today. And one look at the convent does seem to reveal something alarming - all the third-floor shutters on the attic windows are bolted and permanently sealed. Why? Surely not

If you believe the stories, the French Quarter in New Orleans is filled with vampires and blood-suckers of every persuasion.

so that hurricane winds won't rip off the shutters - it must be because it's to keep the vampires shuttered inside. Right?

And the story gets better. In 1978, two would-be investigators requested to see the caskets on the third floor of the convent. The archdiocese - not surprisingly - denied their request. Unwilling to take "no" for an answer, they returned that night, climbed over the wall, and set up recording equipment in the courtyard. The next day, their equipment was found scattered around the property, and the two men were found dead on the porch steps. The murders - if that happened at all, and I've had a tough time documenting that - were never solved.

It's not surprising that the Ursuline nuns became the subjects of such nasty rumors. They were a scandalous bunch - they not only offered the first school in America to teach girls, but they were also the first to offer education to African American children. So, of course, they have been sheltering vampires for 200 years.

New Orleans' most famous "real" vampire is the Comte de Saint-Germain. He was a French alchemist of the eighteenth century who claimed to have the "elixir of life" and often boasted that he was 6,000 years old. He knew more about science and history than most in his time and spoke at least ten languages, along with ancient Greek and Sanskrit. He was also a great storyteller and became a favorite in the court of Louis XV of France. He was invited to many banquets in the finest homes in Paris, but he reportedly never ate a thing. The first record of his suspected immortality was at a party at the mansion of Madame de Pompadour in 1760. An elderly guest assumed that he was the son of Comte de Saint-Germain that she knew back in 1710, but then she discovered that it was the same man she had known 50 years earlier - he just hadn't aged a day.

Decades passed, and Saint-Germain continued to entertain the wealthy and elite of France and the rest of Europe. His talents included the violin, a deep knowledge of medicine, and he was a master painter. The philosopher Voltaire called Saint-Germain "a man who never dies and knows everything."

There were reports that he finally died in Hamburg, Germany, in 1784, and yet, a French noblewoman claimed that she saw him in Paris nine years later in the crowd to witness the beheading of Marie Antoinette. Was it the same man? Or someone who just looked like him?

That's an interesting question considering the mysterious man that came to New Orleans in 1902. Using the name Jacques Saint Germain, he moved into a luxurious building at the corner of Ursulines and Royal. He told people that he had emigrated to the city from the south of France and that he was a descendant of the famous Comte de Saint-Germain.

While very wealthy, Saint Germain never really became part of the community. He wasn't welcomed into the upper-crust society. He was described as charming, very intelligent, a master of languages, and a wonderful guest to have at parties, though - as long as he knew when to exit gracefully at the end of the evening.

In public, Saint Germain seemed to have a different woman on his arm every night. One cold night in December, he picked up a woman in a local pub and brought her home with him. Later that night, she threw herself from a second-story window. As bystanders rushed to help her, they saw that she was covered in blood, and her throat was torn open as if a dog had mauled her. The wound - and all the blood - had not been from the fall. The woman cried that Saint Germain had attacked her. He had rushed at her suddenly, and he'd begun biting her savagely on the neck. She got free, and she jumped from the window. She died later that evening at Charity Hospital.

When New Orleans police officers forced their way into Saint Germain's home to arrest him, he was gone. There was no trace of him other than bloodstains on the wooden floor. He'd packed his things, and he'd vanished, but he left something behind - wine bottles filled with human blood.

One morning in early 1932, a terrified young girl entered the New Orleans police station. She was covered in blood, and her wrists had been cut. She claimed that two men had kidnapped her, tied her up, and then slit her wrists, draining her blood into a cup before drinking it. Then they bandaged her wounds and repeated the ritual for the next three nights. The authorities rushed her to the hospital but not before discovering that she knew the address where the two men lived - 622 St. Ann Street.

The home belonged to the Carter brothers - Wayne and John - and they seemed to have a normal life. They made a living working each day on the docks, unloading fresh seafood - but their nighttime activities were very different. The two men believed they were vampires.

The police rushed to their home and found four victims. Three of them were still alive, and the fourth - a nine-year-old girl -

This building in the French Quarter was said to be home to the Carter Brothers – two real New Orleans vampires

was dead. Hidden in the house, they allegedly found 15 other bodies, all of them drained of blood.

The Carters initially escaped from the trap the police laid for them, but they were eventually captured and executed in the electric chair in 1936. However, over the next several years, the police had more than 20 calls about break-ins in homes across the city. The descriptions of the prowlers matched the Carter brothers.

Legend has it that their tomb was opened, but their coffins were empty.

And that's not all. The stories go on to say that every winter, the brothers return to their old home on St. Ann Street. According to previous owners of the building, they had just purchased it and came home one evening to see two figures standing on the second-floor balcony. They called out to them, and the figures leaped off - and vanished.

Ghosts? Vampires? We may never know - mostly because documentation of these killers is... well, non-existent.

In 1933, the police were called to an alley off Royal Street, where on two consecutive nights, young women, who were assumed to be prostitutes, had their throats torn out. They had been completely drained of blood. The medical examiner believed the bites were human. A witness to one of the assaults claimed that he saw a tall figure effortlessly make his escape by climbing a 12-foot-high fence.

Another popular tale of vampire murders in New Orleans occurred as recently as 1984. There were allegedly nine people found in various spots in the French Quarter - all dead and all with their throats torn out. Eerily, though, there was no blood left at any of the scenes. Officials were dumbfounded, and the cases remain unsolved to this day - but as some storytellers have noted, the locals know the truth.

The New Orleans police are apparently masterfully skilled at keeping these incidents out of the newspapers and out of official reports. The closest thing to these murders that can be found were two unsolved killings in 1978 - but I don't think anyone seriously considered a vampire to be the culprit.

Although, as so many locals will tell you, paranormal incidents like this are hidden in plain sight from city officials because they couldn't handle the truth.

New Orleans seems to have a bit of a problem with the truth when it comes to vampires. As home to the late author Anne Rice, who wrote some of the best books about vampires in existence, the city should probably be recognized more for its fictional bloodsuckers than for the real thing.

There *are* vampires - of a sort -- in New Orleans, and Anne Rice helped to establish the city as the go-to spot for the goth vampire crowd. They became an underground subculture in the city with private clubs, meeting places, fang-makers, and conventions.

They even had their own bar for years, although their influence has faded a bit over the years. In the 1990s, though, if you wanted to meet up with the vampire crowd, you went to the Dungeon on Toulouse Street. It has a foreboding entrance down a dark, narrow alley, and the inside really does feel like a dungeon. The restrooms are hidden behind swinging bookcases to confuse the mortals, and the bar and dance floor can be found upstairs. Music blasts at a level to well... wake the dead.

But just because the sinister vampiric strangers in New Orleans are largely of the imaginative kind, it doesn't mean that America hasn't been home to vampires of one kind or another for more than two centuries.

THE UNDEAD IN NEW ENGLAND

Most of us know the basics of vampire legends. They were the "undead." Described as lean and cadaverous, they were like an old corpse. A vampire had red lips and extended canine teeth. His skin was white, almost transparent, and his flesh was always cold - only warmed after a meal of blood. His eyes gleamed, sometimes flashing red, and his eyebrows were said to meet above his nose. His fingernails were curved like claws, his ears might be pointed, and his breath had the fetid, coppery smell of blood. He was also supernaturally strong, said to have the strength of a dozen or more men.

The vampire as a living corpse was permanently attached to its burial place, or at least to the soil in which he had been buried. One of the many rules that seemed to govern a vampire's behavior was his need to return to his coffin, grave, or tomb before sunrise each morning and sleep in it during the day. Although Hollywood suggested that sunlight could destroy a vampire, folklore said nothing of the kind, only relegated most of the vampire's activities to the nocturnal hours.

Luckily, the vampire's weaknesses were overshadowed by its variety of supernatural powers - not the least of which was his ability, in many tales, to get in and out of a grave through six feet of soil. Hungarian tales gave the vampire the supernatural ability to change into a cloud or mist. There was also the Balkan belief that vampires could control various fearsome animals like wolves or bats.

Occasionally, a few tales would give the vampire himself the ability to change into an animal, like a wolf or a cat. A few Romanian stories mentioned he could transform into a bat. Bats, of course, are nocturnal animals, often associated with dark and evil deeds, so it's not a surprise that it became part of the vampire legend. However, it was rarely mentioned until the nineteenth century, when European travelers began to regularly visit South America - and return with tales about a bat that nourished itself solely on blood. It was promptly named after its human counterpart from folklore and was just as promptly incorporated into vampire stories.

Finally, one of the more useful of the vampire's talents was his hypnotic ability, which enabled him to mesmerize his victims and send them to sleep so that he could feed on them without a struggle. A victim might wake up feeling tired and drained but would remember nothing of the previous night's visitor - perhaps until she saw the two small punctures on the side of her neck.

Perhaps it was another magical power, or perhaps just another rule in vampire lore, but the vampire seemed to have many ways to recruit new bloodsuckers to the ranks. In the most traditional sense, a person could become a vampire after being fed upon and then drinking some of the vampire's blood. This exchange of fluids seemed to be the most reliable method, although some stories claimed that a person who was drained of his blood would rise from the grave after three days as a vampire himself.

But according to the lore, this was, by no means, the only way that you might end up as one of the undead. The old tales stressed most frequently that anyone who died in a state of sin, without the blessings of the Church, risked becoming a vampire; so, did those who were exceedingly wicked or who dabbled in black magic. Balkan legends added that people might return as vampires if they died after perjuring themselves, or were cursed by their parents, committed suicide, or - most prominently - after being excommunicated from the Church. In all these cases, the horror of becoming one of the undead was a punishment for evildoers.

But a man could turn into a vampire through no fault of his own. If his corpse did not receive full funeral rites of the Church, if he died without being baptized or was murdered and his death was never avenged, he might become a vampire. Some were cursed, it was said, by something as simple as a cat jumping over a coffin that had not been buried. If anyone saw the cat perform this act, the transformation of a corpse into a vampire could be prevented with a bit of homemade magic. They simply had to place a piece of iron in the corpse's hand, put a piece of hawthorn in the coffin, or hang a wreath of garlic around the corpse's neck.

Such remedies were expected to protect a person from a vampire, too. But folk magic was not the only thing that was believed to keep vampires away. The Church also helped by offering the protection of holy water, holy relics, and even communion wafers. But given the vampire's evil nature, the best protection was the crucifix, the most powerful symbol of good. Wearing a cross around one's neck was always a good insurance policy, as was clutching a piece of silver, which was universally feared by every kind of evil spirit.

If anyone suspected that a recently buried body might rise again as a vampire, and it was too late to place hawthorn or garlic in the coffin, Slavonic legend suggested thrusting iron skewers straight down into the grave, pinning the vampire into his coffin. It also might be possible to bury a person in question, such as a suicide, under running water to prevent his return as a vampire. Running water had always been considered a barrier to evil creatures and, in some cases, could even kill vampires if they fell into it.

In America, our colonial ancestors were aware of vampires as monsters, death-bringers, and things to be feared. An unsuspecting community that fell under the spell of one of these creatures could very well be destroyed. In historical America, vampires were not mythical creatures from books and folklore - they were unquestionably real.

The stories of vampires in America originated in colonial New England. The influx of various immigrants from Europe - British, Dutch, German, Romanian, and Polish - brought many old traditions to the American shores and created a place where many different beliefs could flourish, develop, and change. The German and Dutch settlers came to the New World with many supernatural creatures that translated to the undead being called back to life. Nearly all of them attacked the living and drank their blood. Such ghoulish traditions blended with Native American myths of nameless creatures that were halfway between some sort of monster and specter. Both the Wampanoag of Massachusetts and the Narragansett of Rhode Island told of a thing that had the form of a man but hid in the shadows of the forest. It would attack hunters and travelers unlucky enough to pass by. No weapon could kill it, and a man had only to speak its name to summon it from the dark woods. Precisely what this creature did with its victims was unknown, but it was unwise to cross its path. It's easy to see how belief in such a being could easily mix with some of the mythology brought to America by the new settlers.

Another element in American vampire mythology was religion. The stern Christianity of the Puritans shaped the lives of New England settlers, and the Devil was everywhere in those days. He was in the forests, the remote valleys, and the dark caves scattered around god-fearing settlements, ready to ensnare the unsuspecting. Their only protection from diabolical attacks was their faith and belief in God. From the earliest days of the Pilgrims in 1620, the colonists framed their world through religion and supernatural intervention. In 1692, when the Massachusetts colony was facing its most serious political and religious crises, their anxiety was expressed not by political activity but through a witchcraft-inspired panic in the village of Salem. It was a perfect example of how the American colonial world was heavily influenced by faith and the signs of evil that were all around them.

In the 1740s, a radical minster named George Whitefield traveled along the American coast, preaching to packed conversations at the start of what came to be called the First Great Awakening. From this period emerged groups with radical theories regarding salvation, sin, and the world. They were the strict Baptists, the Universalists - who denied the existence of Hell - Evangelical Calvinists, and many others.

Some faiths expressed views that were, let's say, a little strange. The early followers of the minister Edward Browne, for instance, believed the Devil was a woman and, consequently, no woman could enter heaven. Saintly women were turned into men at the time of death.

Mother Anne Lee's Shakers, who had fled England in 1774, believed that lust was the Original Sin, so any contact between men and women was forbidden.

A Perfectionist named Shadrack Ireland believed that the "second coming" of Christ was imminent, and he instructed his followers to place themselves on stone slabs in sealed underground chambers beneath the Massachusetts hills. That way, when the trumpet sounded, they could walk out, whole and ready to meet God.

For many of the faithful, sin and evil - and the avoidance of both - became serious preoccupations. Once a man had given his life to God, the Devil would stop at nothing to destroy him. The Devil's agents were everywhere. The Native Americans who lived in the woods were often described in the writings of ministers of the era as "worshippers of the Devil." When Indians attacked their settlements, it was unquestionably the work of Satan. And God permitted these atrocities to occur because of the sins of the colonists, whether real or imagined. Such raids were punishment for the colonists and a powerful reminder of the evil that lurked in the shadowy corners of the new land.

On May 19, 1780, a spectacular event shook New England to its core and galvanized many radical churches. It was already a time of religious fervor as itinerant preachers traveled among the people, preaching of sin and the presence of evil. Then, at mid-day on May 19, the sky suddenly went dark, and the sun disappeared, forcing lamps and candles to be lit. What caused the famous "New England's Dark Day" is unknown, but it was terrifying. While undoubtedly some sort of strange, natural phenomenon, the religious felt there could only be one explanation - Judgement Day had arrived. The darkness lasted until around midnight, and when it finally dispersed, the stars could be seen shining above. The world had not come to an end.

The effect on New England's religious community, however, was electric. If the darkness was not a sign of Christ's return, then it had to be something else, perhaps even more dire. Many said that it was a warning from God that America was a place of sin. It was a hint of things to come if men did not mend their ways and follow the word of the Lord. In many places in New England, everything was treated as a sign from God or evidence of the Devil's work. Satan was stepping up his efforts to bring ruin and damnation to America, and, as if to prove it, many local villages and towns experienced epidemics of typhoid fever and smallpox in the months that followed.

Fear, myth, rumor, and religion all combined to create the legends of American vampires, but perhaps the greatest element of the emerging mythology was disease. The conditions under which the settlers lived were poor and unsanitary. Many of them lived on the edges of lakes, bogs, and swamps, which were perfect breeding grounds for all sorts of ailments, most of them fatal. Epidemics of various kinds swept through the colonies, claiming the lives of the weak and vulnerable as they did so. Once again, thanks to the religious fervor of the time, epidemics were regarded as another sign of God's judgment upon a sinful people. Typhoid and tuberculosis flourished through the colonies, along with many forms of respiratory and lung infections. It was not uncommon for entire families - even entire towns - to sometimes be lost to a single epidemic.

One of the first writers to connect the stories of vampires with disease was an anthropologist named George R. Stetson.

He wrote an article called "The Animistic Vampire of New England" for the *American Anthropologist Journal* in January 1896. He wrote of many places in New England where a belief in vampires still flourished thanks to isolation and poverty. He made a connection between epidemics and the belief that vampires preyed on families.

Between about 1780 and the latter part of the 1800s, plagues of typhoid, smallpox, and tuberculosis claimed many lives in small communities already devastated by poverty and a decline in the agriculture that had once been the lifeblood of the town. Poor diet and harsh life often took their toll on the more vulnerable, making them easy victims of all sorts of contagions. Perhaps looking for an explanation for the lives that were ruined, vampires were blamed. In Stetson's writings, he mentioned a curious custom that had started to occur following the outbreaks of disease. Bodies of victims were exhumed and examined, and, in many cases, hearts and some internal organs were burned to prevent the corpse from coming back to claim the lives of other family members.

It's easy to understand how tuberculosis came to be connected to something that drained the lives of its victims. Consumption, as it was usually known then, was the great plague of the nineteenth century. In New England alone, death tolls were staggering. The illness was spread by everyday living conditions - large families, often poorly nourished, shared living space for long periods. It was common for the disease to run through entire families. Highly contagious and generally fatal, tuberculosis was so lethal that doctors called it the first disease "to deter practitioners from attempting a cure."

As consumption claimed life after life, it began to be called the "White Death." It was a fitting nickname. As the disease progressed, the body was transformed from its previous ruddy complexion to the skin becoming stark white, almost ghostly,

Tuberculosis, or "consumption" as it was often called, was the great plague of the nineteenth century, wiping out entire families and, sometimes, entire communities.

and translucently thin. A network of light blue veins became visible beneath the surface. Victims often ran fevers, which caused their cheeks to become reddened. They had difficulty breathing and developed a terrible cough that often brought up bloody phlegm. There were often fainting spells, anemia, weight loss, and an increasingly fragile demeanor. The thin, pale, weak, and listless victims often came to resemble a living corpse. Oddly, due to the romantic and beauty standards of the time, these symptoms made the victims, especially young women, strangely alluring. As the illness progressed, they became more beautiful - while their bodies, health, and strength were consumed by the incurable disease.

It was probably easy for early New Englanders to imagine this wasting away - the process of being consumed by the disease - as the result of a vampire preying on the very life of the victim. No doubt, to some, the resulting mysteriously heightened feminine beauty was evidence of a transformation from victim to vampire. A seemingly bizarre component of the disease contributed to the illusion - consumptives occasionally experienced surprising periods of manic energy. Many were known to have powerful sex drives. Some have suggested that these attributes proved that the individuals were clinging to life in a manner that could survive the grave.

At some point in New England's history, it came to be accepted that when someone died of consumption, they could come back from the dead and drain the life from their surviving relatives. To stop this, family members opened their graves and attempted to kill them again. When relatives opened the coffins of the recently deceased consumptives, the corpses, formerly thin and frail, were often found to be bloated and engorged. Fingernails seemed to have grown into claws, and perhaps the most damning evidence was blood often found in the mouth. There were even some accounts of bodies jerking and gurgling as the remains were being mutilated.

Of course, all of this "evidence" of vampirism could be explained scientifically in these modern times. The body's decomposition caused it to bloat, the flesh receded from the fingers, making the nails look as though they had grown, and a loss of tissue in the lungs from the disease caused blood to remain in the mouth. At that time, though, those who looked for it easily found "proof" that the dead person was a vampire.

But driving a wooden stake through the heart of the vampire was not practiced by New Englanders. That was a European tradition. Instead, the technique to destroy the monster was to remove its heart and burn it. Decapitation was also popular, as were other mutilations of the body. In each case, disturbing the body seemed to bring the trouble to an end - and it kept the dead from leaving the grave.

One of the earliest stories of a vampire in New England was recorded in Manchester, Vermont, and dates to the late eighteenth century. The account was discovered in the personal papers of Judge John S. Pettibone and was written down at some point between 1857 and 1872.

The story, by all accounts, was true.

The events began on March 8, 1789, when Captain Isaac Burton married a beautiful young woman named Rachel Harris. She was from a prominent family in the region, and the Manchester community praised the marriage. The captain seemed to have found the perfect partner, but unfortunately, the marriage did not last long. Shortly after the wedding, Rachel's health began to fail. Consumption was prevalent in the area, and Rachel succumbed to it, dying slowly and painfully. Less than one year after she married Isaac Burton, she died on February 1, 1790.

Captain Burton was distraught over the death of his young wife, and he mourned her for many months. After nearly a year had passed, he decided to marry again. He took a new bride, Hulda Powell, daughter of a wealthy landowner, on January 4, 1791. Hulda was described as a lovely, fit, and healthy young woman - but she didn't stay that way for long.

A few months into the marriage, Hulda began to display symptoms of the same wasting disease that had taken Rachel. Her vitality faded away, she became unnaturally pale, and she developed a harsh, bloody cough. Desperate to save his second wife from death, Burton spent huge sums of money on her treatment, bringing in physicians from large cities to investigate his wife's condition. Although they offered opinions and prescribed tonics, they were of little use, and soon Hulda was confined to her bed, just as Rachel had been. The stories say that she became delusional in her illness, claiming that she saw Rachel in her room, her mouth covered in blood and smelling of dirt. The stories frightened Burton and his in-laws, and they took turns staying with her at night, looking after her, and perhaps protecting her from her delusions. As time passed, Hulda continued to deteriorate.

One of the relatives who sat beside Hulda's bed was an elderly aunt who was well-versed in the region's folklore. She listened to her niece's tales of late-night visitations from a ghastly-looking Rachel Harris and talk turned to vampires. She offered Isaac a rather chilling explanation for what was ailing his sickly wife. Bluntly, she told him that she believed his late wife was draining the life from Hulda's body. The only way to stop it was to remove the body of Rachel from her grave and burn it. After that, Hulda had a chance to recover, but, even then, recovery was not certain. It was certain that if nothing were done at all, though, Hulda would surely die - and soon, the vampire would prey on other members of the family.

Frightened and at a loss, Burton approached an old friend and town selectman named Timothy Mead to request the exhumation of Rachel's body. Mead refused, telling his friend that vampires were only a superstition. Rachel had been a respectable young woman from a good family, and she didn't deserve to be connected to such nonsense. The matter was put aside, and Hulda grew weaker with each passing day. The old aunt's beliefs seemed to be supported by her decline, especially after Hulda began to complain of feeling a pressing weight on her chest at night, as though someone was sitting on it. In addition, she now had flecks of blood around the sides of her mouth, as if someone had been taking it from her body. Each night, Burton and several relatives remained by the young woman's bed, only to be startled from sleep by Hulda's cries and screams that Rachel was in the room with her.

Rumors began to spread around town, and whispers about a vampire began to be heard from every corner. Of course, the progress of tuberculosis in the body will produce a variety of symptoms, from coughing up blood to respiratory problems that might feel as if the victim is being suffocated to pale skin and feverish dreams. All Hulda's ailments could be attributed to the disease, but to Captain Burton and many of the people in Manchester, the symptoms only meant one thing - a vampire was at work.

Burton approached Timothy Mead again, and this time, aware of the rising tide of rumor and fear in town, Mead arranged for an exhumation. On a February morning in 1793, Rachel's coffin was removed from the cemetery and taken to the local blacksmith's shop. Despite their fear, a crowd gathered to watch the events. Once opened, the casket revealed a bloated corpse that was scarcely recognizable as the young and beautiful Rachel Harris. Around her mouth were dark stains of blood, which were noticed immediately by the crowd. The body was so bloated, the onlookers said, because it was engorged with blood. It was incontrovertible evidence that Rachel was indeed a vampire.

Her heart, lungs, and liver were removed and were cast into the searing heat of the blacksmith's forge. According to the account, the stench that came from the burning organs was nearly overpowering, and several onlookers later declared that they heard the sigh of a woman as the black smoke curled up into the sky. Others claimed they saw what looked like a black serpent slither upward in the smoke and vanish as it began to disperse.

If Isaac Burton expected his wife to recover after the gruesome task at the blacksmith shop, he was extremely disappointed. Hulda was too weakened by her illness and did not survive. She died on September 6, 1793, and despite some initial fears that she might return from the grave as Rachel did, nothing was ever heard from her again.

The story of Rachel Harris Burton, the wife who returned from the grave to take a blood and wasting sort of revenge on her successor, spread wildly throughout New England. It reinforced old beliefs, not only about vampires but about the presence of evil in the land and about the necessity of living a good and proper life. All over the region, the tale became a staple of local folklore and would be revisited many times over the century to come.

Within three years of the exhumation of Rachel Burton, another vampire account reared its ugly head in New England. This tale took place in Cumberland, Rhode Island, and involved the death of a young woman named Abigail Staples, who died near the end of 1793 at the age of only 23. It was believed that she died from consumption, but unfortunately, her deathbed was not the last time that her family would see her.

On February 8, 1796, Abigail's father, a prosperous merchant named Stephen Staples, approached the Cumberland town council with an unusual request - he wanted to dig up the body of his dead daughter. In what he described as an "experiment," he wished to exhume Abigail, who had died several months before, to see if this might save the life of his other daughter, Lavinia.

Abigail had been a moody, unhappy girl who, while never married, often dreamed of a husband and children. When her sister married a young man named Stephen Chace, it was believed that Abigail harbored deep resentment toward the marriage. Her own dreams of matrimony were cut short by consumption, and she died.

Shortly after her sister's death, Lavinia exhibited similar symptoms, and her health deteriorated. She was confined to her bed for a time, and, as she slept, she had visions of a dark figure crouched at the end of her bed. It jumped onto her chest, crushing her with its weight and stealing the breath from her body. Her family assumed that the dreams would pass with the sickness, but then one morning, her husband was very disturbed when she sat upright in bed and cried out a single word - "Abigail."

Stephen was troubled by her outburst and went to see his father-in-law. Staples listened to what the young man said. He knew the legends of vampires but had never put much faith in the stories. However, the incident occurred at an interesting time. Several people in the area were also suffering from tuberculosis. In keeping with the religious fervor of the times, several local ministers had proclaimed that the illness was God's punishment on his wayward people. The Devil was near at hand, they said, and would soon make his presence known. Staples was a man who took his faith seriously, and so he decided to take his son-in-law's concerns to the authorities.

The members of the town council reacted with skepticism. While they were sympathetic toward the girl's grieving father and husband, they believed that vampires belonged in the realm of folklore and ignorant superstition. But they were also acutely aware of the sermons being given by ministers in the area and how they had stirred up notions of ever-present devils and demons. Sensing their uncertainty about how to proceed, Staples pressed the issue, saying that if the Devil was close at hand, then vampires might be among them, too. Stephen Chace then made his own impassioned plea, suggesting that it would be for the good of the community to dispel the terror that gripped so many people. Abigail's corpse should be exhumed and inspected and, if nothing were amiss, the girl would be reburied with decency. Somewhat reluctantly, the council authorized the exhumation. They only had one stipulation - the "experiment" had to be kept as secret as possible, and no written record of it could be made.

In keeping with the council's request, Staples, Chace, and three hired men went out to a small graveyard on the Staples' property. They arrived after nightfall, lanterns in hand, and unearthed Abigail's body. No record exists about what they found, but local legend recalls that whatever young Stephen Chace saw when the coffin was opened that night almost drove him mad. He wandered the countryside, muttering to himself until sunrise. Stephen Staples never again spoke of that night or what he had witnessed, but he was a changed man after that. For the rest of his life, he was troubled by horrible nightmares. Legend also claims that one of the workmen who unearthed the coffin committed suicide a short time later.

What became of Lavinia Chace is unknown. She simply vanished from history after that. She might have recovered, or she, too, might have perished from consumption. There is no marker to identify her grave to say when or how she died, and no mention is made of her in any subsequent account.

There is no record of any similar occurrences in the region, and it is unclear if any similar deaths took place in the wake of Abigail's demise. However, a curious headstone was erected nearby for a man named Simon Whipple Aldrich. It can be found in the Union Cemetery Annex, and it bears a very odd inscription: "Although consumption's vampire grasp had seized thy mortal frame."

The graves of Simon Aldrich and his wife, Marietta. Simon's stone contains the epitaph, "Although consumption's vampire grasp had seized thy mortal frame."

Simon Aldrich was the youngest son of Colonel Dexter Aldrich and his wife, Margery. He died on May 6, 1841, presumably of tuberculosis. However, the strange mention of the word vampire in the inscription has intrigued historians over the years. Why was it included on the headstone? It may, of course, be only a turn of phrase, but it may also be a reminder of the dark days of Abigail Staples - and perhaps proof of the indelible mark that she left on the community.

Stutley Tillinghast was a prosperous apple farmer who lived in Exeter, Rhode Island. He was liked and admired in the community and was active in the local church. He was a good provider, probably everyone in town agreed, and he was an excellent father. He and his wife, Honor, were parents to 14 children, and all of them, against the odds in those days, had survived into early adulthood.

Then one night, the farmer awoke after an unsettling and disturbing dream. The nightmare was especially vivid and had left him in a cold sweat. He dreamed that he was walking between the rows of his apple orchard. On one side, the trees were healthy; their limbs weighed down by an abundance of fruit. On the other side of the orchard, the trees had withered and died. The branches had dropped their leaves, and rotten apples lay scattered about on the ground. Somewhere, in the dark shadows of the dream orchard, he heard the voice of his daughter, Sarah, calling to him. As he turned to see where she was, a cold wind blew through the trees and chilled him to the bone. Branches creaked in the trees, and dry leaves swirled about his feet, scraping and rustling. The voice faded, and as it did, the stench of decay spread from the diseased side of the orchard, and he knew that half of his crop had been lost. Tillinghast awoke with a terrible feeling of dread. He was sure the dream was some sort of portent of things to come - but of what?

Fearing that the dream predicted something terrible about that year's apple harvest, the farmer was greatly relieved when it was successful as always. He thought about the nightmare for a short while longer, but then his fear began to fade as the family settled in for the winter.

A short time later, though, Sarah, the couple's oldest daughter, grew sick. Sarah had always been a moody young woman, preferring to stay in her room and read and wander alone in the woods instead of spending time with the rest of the family. At first, no one noticed when she began to skip meals or stay in bed a little longer than usual. But as she became weaker and grew pale and sickly, her mother realized that she was terribly ill. At the end of 1799, she died. The cause was, of course, given as "consumption," and she was laid to rest in the family plot, a short distance from the Tillinghast house.

But it was soon believed that she had returned from the grave.

A few weeks after Sarah's death, the Tillinghast's youngest son, James, came down to breakfast one morning looking pale and shaken. He claimed that his chest hurt badly, "where Sarah touched him." His mother assured him that it had only been a bad dream, and yet she could hear an unhealthy rattle in his lungs. He was sent back to bed with a stack of blankets to keep him warm. In the nights that followed, he continued to claim that Sarah came to visit him in the night and would often touch him. He grew sicker, and his parents assumed that the stories resulted from his fevers, no matter how real they seemed to the boy. He didn't have bad dreams for long, though. James followed his sister to the grave.

A short time later, another of the Tillinghast girls, Andris, became sick. Her sister, Ruth, also began wasting away. Both girls died, and their parents began to fear that God had turned against their family. Before the girls died, they repeatedly complained about their dead sister Sarah and claimed that she was coming to them in the night. They said she came as a ghostly figure, entering the room through the window. Sarah would then come to the side of the bed and push down on each girl's chest, making it difficult for her to breathe.

More of the Tillinghast children weakened and died in the days and weeks that followed. The fifth child, Hannah, was married and lived several miles away with her husband. She often visited her parents and helped Honor with the daily chores. On several nights, though, after leaving the Tillinghast farm, she was convinced she was being followed. One night, she caught a glimpse of someone in the shadows and thought it was her sister, Sarah - but Sarah was dead. Oddly, she had dreams that Sarah was in her bedroom with her that night. A short time later, Hannah grew sick and began wasting away. She died in the spring of 1800.

By the time Hannah died, Stutley Tillinghast had begun to recall the strange dream that he had experienced about the apple orchard. In this vision, exactly half of the orchard had withered and died. He finally realized what the dream had been trying to tell him. In despair, he realized that seven of his children were going to die. He didn't try to ponder the supernatural meanings behind the dream, however. At this point, he was trying to puzzle out the meaning behind his children's complaints about nighttime visits from Sarah. Before each of them died, they claimed their sister came into their room at night. What could this mean?

Another death followed, and then the seventh Tillinghast child, Ezra, also began to complain of strange feelings of fatigue and of seeing Sarah in his room at night. He died soon after.

And then, Honor began to weaken - and dream of Sarah coming to her in the darkness, too.

The Tillinghast family plot, where Sarah and other members of the family were buried. Sarah's father believed that she had returned from the grave.

After talking it over with some of his neighbors, Tillinghast began to believe that Sarah was responsible for the string of deaths in his family. Knowing the only way to save the rest of them was to take action, Stutley, along with two of his hired men, made his way to the cemetery where the body of Sarah had been buried. They took along shovels, ropes, and a flask of oil.

Throughout the night, the men unearthed the coffins of all the Tillinghast children. All of them had been in the earth for more than six months when the caskets were opened. They found the bodies to be rotting and decayed - except for one. Sarah's body, it was said, was in perfect condition. She was lying as if in repose. Her hair and nails had grown, her flesh was soft and supple, and her eyes were open, staring up into the sky. When the coffin lid was removed, and one of the workmen looked down on her face, he immediately fell to his knees and began to pray.

When Tillinghast saw his daughter, he was seized with horror, and he rushed to the wagon and returned with the can of oil. Taking a large knife from his belt, he bent down into the coffin and cut open Sarah's chest. Her heart and liver were sliced out, and Tillinghast doused them with oil and set them on fire. A sharp stench filled the air as they burned, and the men watched as the smoke curled into the air above the burial ground. The organs turned to ash, and the men, still shaking, judged that the danger was past. They reburied all the coffins and left the cemetery as the sun began to rise.

Honor Tillinghast survived her illness, recovered her health, and later bore her husband two more children. All the remaining children outlived their parents. In Tillinghast's vision, half of his orchard was lost to an unexplainable scourge, just as half of his children had been. The eerie dream had come true.

MERCY BROWN

The story of New England's last vampire, Mercy Brown, is a shadow that still lingers over Rhode Island today. Even though the story came to a cruel and bloody end in 1892, it had its beginnings years before, in 1883, when consumption was claiming lives in the area around Exeter.

George Brown was a hard-working farmer who prospered in this part of southern Rhode Island, not far from Providence. He and his wife, Mary Eliza, had raised six children and lived a comfortable but simple life. In late 1883, the first in a series of terrible events occurred on the Brown farm when Mary began to show the telltale signs of having contracted consumption. The sturdy, once healthy woman began to suffer from fainting spells and periods of weakness. Most of all, she was gripped with a harsh cough that kept her awake through the night. After these horrible fits of coughing, the handkerchief she kept pressed to her mouth would be covered in blood. The disease began to ravage her body, and on December 8, she slipped into unconsciousness and did not awaken. She died at the age of only 36.

Seven months later, the Browns' oldest daughter, 20-year-old Mary Olive, also came down with the dreaded illness. She developed the now familiar symptoms of weight loss, weakness, and a wracking cough. Mary Olive grew paler and weaker with each passing day, and on June 6, 1884, she followed her mother to the grave.

Several years of peace followed the death of Mary Olive, and during this time, Edwin -- George and Mary's only son -- got married and bought his own farm in nearby West Wickford. He hoped to make a life for himself and his new bride while he worked in a store to support his family and save money for the future. All was going well until 1891, when Edwin noticed the symptoms of the disease that had killed his sister and mother. He resigned from his job and moved west to Colorado Springs, following advice from friends. The city had begun to develop a reputation for helping ease consumption patients' suffering, and Edwin hoped the nearby mineral waters and the drier climate might restore his health.

While Edwin and his wife were out west, things took a dark turn for the Brown family in Exeter. In January 1892, Edwin received word that his 19-year-old sister, Mercy, had also become sick and died. Her consumption was diagnosed as the "galloping" variety, and she quickly passed away and was entombed in the receiving vault at Chestnut Hill Cemetery in Exeter.

Meanwhile, Edwin realized that his health was not improving in Colorado. He and his wife decided that they should return home so that Edwin could spend the remainder of his days with family, friends, and loved ones. They made the journey back to Rhode Island and moved in with Edwin's in-laws.

By the time Edwin returned to Rhode Island, his father was in a dreadful and worried state. Friends were convinced that the family was being preyed on by a vampire and suggested that Brown should exhume the bodies of the other family members and see which one of them it was. While upset and worried, he refused to go along with such nonsense. It was superstitious fear, and he would not be a party to it.

But one of Brown's younger friends - his identity was never documented - took matters into his own hands. He decided to pay a visit to Dr. Harold Metcalf, who was not only the district medical examiner but also the physician who had treated Mercy during her illness, and ask for his help. He told him that Edwin was also suffering from the same disease and several friends and neighbors believed the only way in which his life could be saved was to have the bodies of his mother and two sisters exhumed to ascertain if the heart of any of the bodies still contained blood. If any of them did, then that dead body was feeding off Edwin's living tissue and blood. Metcalf considered this as absurd as George Brown did and sent the young man away.

At some point over the next week, Brown's friends finally convinced him of the possibility that one of the dead women was indeed a vampire. Perhaps, only because he had exhausted all his other options, Brown agreed to the exhumation - but only if Dr. Metcalf would also attend. The young man who had previously gone to see the doctor returned to his door. He told him that George Brown, though not believing in the superstition himself, wanted to pacify his friends by opening the graves. Because of this, he asked Dr. Metcalf if he would attend and perform the autopsies. Dr. Metcalf again balked at the idea but eventually agreed to go along, realizing that he could not persuade them from what they believed was their duty.

On the cold morning of March 17, 1892, a group of men marched down Purgatory Road to the Chestnut Hill Cemetery.

Their goal was to save the life of Edwin Brown. To do that, they would have to take part in a macabre ritual - a "certain cure" for vampire victims that had been written about in 1784 by a Willington County, Connecticut resident named Moses Holmes. The "cure" required that the body of a dead relative is disinterred and that any part of the deceased that is not decomposed be burned and then consumed by the victim. By searching the graves of Brown family members who had already died, Edwin's friends and family members believed that they might find the culprit leading the young man into his own early grave.

George Brown had buried his wife and his two daughters and now realized that if he didn't do something, his son might be lost to him, as well. George had initially put no stock in the ghoulish superstition that some claimed might save Edwin's life. As time passed, though, he was at last convinced to allow the ritual to proceed. He loved his son and planned to accompany him to the cemetery that morning, but at the last moment, he balked at the idea of exhuming the graves of the three women. If one of them truly was a vampire, he could not face it.

The group of would-be vampire hunters carried with them a collection of picks and shovels for the grim work ahead. The body of Edwin's sister, Mercy, would be the easiest to obtain. She had died only two months earlier, on January 12, and her body had been placed inside of a stone receiving crypt on the cemetery grounds so that she could be buried when the ground began to thaw for the season.

The old stone receiving vault at Chestnut Hill Cemetery in Exeter, Rhode Island

The exhumation that occurred that day might have never come to public attention if the family did not seek out an official sanction for their plan from Dr. Metcalf. He "acted under protest, as it were being an unbeliever," stated a letter about the incident that appeared in a local newspaper. The doctor was an intelligent young man who didn't believe Edwin's illness had anything to do with a vampire. He did all that he could to discourage the exhumation, but since it was not technically against the law, there was little he could do.

By the time Metcalf arrived at the cemetery, the bodies of Mary Brown and her daughter, Mary Olive, had already been unearthed. The men had worked hard to break through the cold and unforgiving earth.

Both corpses were found, after the passages of years, to be in states of advanced decomposition. Mary had been in the ground for almost nine years at this point, and she was in an advanced state of decay. Some of her muscles and flesh remained in a mummified state, but there were no signs of blood in her heart. The men then opened the coffin of Mary Olive, who had also died years before. According to a newspaper account, only a skeleton and a thick growth of hair remained. Dr. Metcalf stated with certainty that they were "just what might be expected from a similar examination of almost any person after the same length of time."

There was no question that they had rested in peace during the past nine years. Neither of the two women could be the vampire that was draining the life from young Edwin.

But there was one coffin left - that of Mercy Brown.

The stone receiving crypt was located at the edge of the cemetery. It was a triangular-shaped building with a heavy wooden door usually kept locked. One of the men had obtained the keys from the sexton this morning, and the door was opened to reveal a dark, damp interior. The cool smell of earth rushed out at them as they stood in the doorway, allowing their eyes to adjust to the darkness within. Mercy's casket was carried from the crypt and out into the sickly sunlight of the overcast morning. The hasp was broken, and the lid was raised.

Her coffin was placed on a small cart inside the tomb. Dr. Metcalf looked inside and began a quick autopsy of the corpse. He noted some signs of decay and the marks left by consumption on her lungs. This did not convince him that she was a vampire, so he finished his examination and announced his findings to the men who had gathered to see to the gruesome tasks at hand. Metcalf told them that nothing was amiss with the body, but they didn't see things the same way he did. When he was unable to convince them, he left the cemetery.

To the other men - and perhaps even to Edwin, who was present for the exhumations - Mercy seemed relatively intact, or at least more so than she should be after being dead for two months. Besides, they were also sure that her body had moved. She had been laid to rest on her back, and somehow the corpse was now resting on its side. Could she have left the casket? Dr. Metcalf, they believed, was simply trying to protect his reputation as a man of science and wanted no part of vampires.

The grave of Mercy Brown – America's most famous "real" vampire

The men were suspicious that something was wrong with Mercy Brown, and what happened next convinced them entirely. One of the men opened her heart with his knife and was startled to see fresh blood come pouring out of the organ. It was quickly removed from her chest. They also cut out her liver because, even though it contained no fresh blood, it was in a remarkably preserved state. The organs were burned, and then the ashes were gathered to make a tonic that would hopefully cure Edwin of the disease.

Edwin consumed the macabre mixture, but it did him little good. On May 2, he joined his mother and sisters in death and was buried at Chestnut Hill. While his death was tragic, all was not lost. He became the last of the Brown family to die from consumption - or the ravages of a vampire, depending on what you believe.

The exhumations, autopsies, and burnings designed to save the living of New England from being consumed by the dead ended with Mercy Brown.

The germs that caused tuberculosis had been discovered in 1882 and the fact that the disease was contagious was established not long afterward. The discovery dismissed the superstitious belief that the illness was caused by vampires that fed on the living, but news of such discoveries was slow in arriving at places like rural New England. Even if the Brown family and their friends heard such accounts, the claim that consumption was caused by invisible organisms passed from one person to another would have seemed perhaps even more unlikely than the idea that people weakened and died after being preyed upon by a monster.

The accounts of the Mercy Brown exhumation had a brief life in the newspapers of the day, all of which seemed more focused on pointing out the superstitious ignorance of country folk than in studying the effects the old folklore had on the lives and deaths of the people involved. Mercy was finally placed in her grave soon after the incident, but that was not the end of her story. Mercy Brown lived on, not only in Rhode Island legend but in other ways, as well.

Author H.P. Lovecraft wrote a horror story called "The Shunned House" in 1924, and it was first published in the October 1937 issue of *Weird Tales* magazine. While not the primary focus of the story, the 1892 exhumation is mentioned when Lovecraft refers to the Exeter "rustics" and even names one of the characters in the story, Mercy. Lovecraft relished New England folklore and legends and incorporated many of them into his stories.

A more important appearance of Mercy Brown in literature occurred in 1897 when the story of her exhumation was used in an altered form for Bram Stoker's novel, *Dracula*. When Stoker died, his years of collected articles and book materials were sold. Among them was the material he used to research his groundbreaking vampire novel. Among the material were clippings about Mercy Brown. He used the bare facts of the story to create the staking of Lucy Westerna by Dr. Van Helsing and his group of vampire hunters in the story - earning Mercy Brown a place in vampire literature history.

To this day, Mercy Brown has not been forgotten by the people of Rhode Island. She retains a place of honor as the last New England vampire, and she casts a long shadow that stretches back to a time when vampires and consumption were both a part of everyday life. Over the years, tuberculosis claimed many more victims than so-called "vampires" ever did, but the end result for both was the same.

Both were conquered by science.

Or were they?

The story of Mercy Brown did not end the stories of real-life vampires in America. They have continued for well over a century, offering vampires of a very different kind.

WHERE VAMPIRES STILL WALK

Traditional vampire stories are not common in American history. European vampires, the blood-sucking monsters of nightmare tales, do not often appear in the stories that were told in the American colonies. In this country, they were usually seen as "death bringers" and, as mentioned, carried disease more than they went around drinking blood. Regardless, vampires were quite real to the early settlers and were monsters to be feared.

Most of the ghastly stories that we have of vampiric attackers are ripped from the true crime headlines and concern people who believe they are vampires, or at least pretend they are. They dress in black, consume blood, or even go as far as to commit cannibalism. There's' nothing mysterious about them. They are usually sick or deluded individuals driven to murder by their mental illnesses.

But there are a few stories - and they are always unsettling.

In the middle and late 1970s, a mysterious figure began to be reported around St. Casimir's Cemetery on the South Side of Chicago, Illinois. The first sighting occurred in 1978 when a man was driving past the cemetery on Pulaski Road  one night and spotted a figure standing just inside the cemetery fence, wearing a long, black cape. The figure had its back to the driver, but he slowed his car to get a better look. As he did, the man behind the gate turned around to face him, revealing a ghastly white face above the neck of the cloak. The sinister-looking figure bared his teeth at the driver, and the man in the car understandably sped off.

On June 14 and 15, the figure was seen again, this time by neighborhood teenagers, who added that he was not only wearing the long cape but also had a top hat on his head. He seemingly vanished without explanation whenever he was approached. The local police believed that the macabre antics of the man were nothing more than a prank to frighten the local children. They became concerned after reports stated that the man had approached, chased, and threatened people on two separate occasions. According to the accounts, the man was "six feet tall, extremely thin with broken teeth and wearing dirty, muddy clothing." Both reports also said that he had a "disgusting odor" to go along with the hat, cape, and makeup - if it was actually makeup, that is.

Stories began to make the rounds about the sightings. Nearly two dozen people traveling southbound on Kostner Avenue near the cemetery arrived at the stoplight at 111th Street with their headlights illuminating the front gates of the cemetery.

Motorists often claimed to see a thin man with a pale face, dressed in black and wearing a cape, peering out at them from the graveyard. Before the traffic light changed, the man apparently disappeared.

Others claimed to be walking or riding a bicycle past the gates and stated they saw the same figure. Some even added that they heard a menacing hiss or a growl before the "vampire" disappeared. A few noted that he would reach out at them through the gate, his fingers curling into claws.

One of the most frightening encounters with the "St. Casimir's Vampire" occurred in 1979 when a woman was driving south on 115th Street, approaching the railroad tracks on the western edge of Restvale Cemetery. She stated later that a man who matched the earlier, vampire-like descriptions suddenly appeared on the street in front of her car. To avoid hitting the man, she swerved into oncoming traffic and then veered back into her lane. She immediately stopped and looked in the rearview mirror, but the man was gone. There was no place that he could have gone, she insisted. He simply vanished.

Another encounter took place in the backyard of an older woman who lived near the cemetery. She opened the sliding patio door of her home to let her dog outside but no sooner had the poodle stepped out when it began to bark loudly. Startled, the woman switched on the back patio light to see what was bothering the dog and was terrified to see a figure lying in the grass. He immediately turned, and she got a long look at his white face and bared teeth. He let out a loud hiss and then got up and began to run. According to her statement, he escaped from her yard by jumping over a four-foot fence without even touching it. When he landed on the other side, he disappeared into the darkness.

Who was this strange creature, and why did he appear near the cemetery gates? No one knew then or has ever offered a credible explanation for his behavior since that time.

In 1981, the small former mining town of Mineral Point, Wisconsin, had a vampire problem. Calls began coming into the local police station on March 14 from people reporting a man, at least six-and-a-half feet tall with a white face and wearing a black cape, lurking in Graceland Cemetery. Skeptical at first, officers were soon convinced that something weird was going on by the sheer number of calls they received.

On March 30, Officer John Pepper responded to the latest call of the "vampire," as he'd been dubbed, and found the "huge person" who was "about 6 feet, 5 and ugly" lurking behind some tombstones in the cemetery. Pepper approached the figure and asked him what he was doing. Whoever the strange man was, he said nothing but immediately turned and began to run. He quickly outdistanced the officer, and when the figure jumped over a four-foot barbed wire fence in a single bound, Pepper called off the chase.

The "vampire" vanished into the darkness.

Soon after, the department stationed extra officers around the cemetery, but it didn't seem to help. The town was abuzz with "vampire fever." Over the next several nights, the police were inundated with sightings of creepy figures in the graveyard and throughout the community. It didn't help that many of the locals started showing up in bars on weekends dressed as vampires.

But the "real" vampire of Graceland Cemetery had disappeared. Eventually, the excitement died out, and the "Mineral Point Vampire" story faded away.

Or it would have if he - or someone a lot like him - wouldn't have returned.

More than two decades later, in March 2004, the police responded to reports of a pale man, dressed all in black, sitting in a tree outside of an apartment complex in Mineral Point, yelling out to the tenants. When officers arrived, the man fled. One of the police officers followed for a short distance, but he quickly lost sight of the tall, thin, and fast-moving individual.

When the other officers caught up with him, the men followed the mysterious man's footprints in the snow until they ended - at the base of an eight-foot stone wall.

In 2008, he was back. On July 11, two Mineral Point residents, 22-year-old Brandon Heinz and his 19-year-old girlfriend Jamie Marker were fishing off a jetty at Ludden Lake around 10:00 p.m. It was an ordinary night until they started hearing noises underneath the dock, "like something was using the boards of the jetty like a ladder, climbing along underneath us."

Brandon began stomping on the boards, believing it was an animal he could scare away. He aimed his flashlight between the wooden slats on the dock, and then he and Jamie heard splashing on the other side of them. Brandon turned his flashlight to see "a figure with dark hair and a very pale face pulling itself up onto the jetty."

The couple watched in shock as the figure rose to its feet - and Jamie ran for their car. Brandon said he felt frozen in place as he looked at the man. He described him as tall, thin, and pale and "wearing some kind of Dracula looking cape and a suit, sort of." Jamie would later describe the figure the same way.

When Brandon finally got a hold of himself, he threw his flashlight at the man and ran up the path to the parked car where Jamie waited, with the windows up and the doors locked. Brandon got into the driver's seat and cranked the ignition. The engine roared to life, and in a panic, he slammed his foot down on the gas pedal. As the tires chewed up the gravel, Jamie looked out the passenger window and saw the man was coming up the path toward them. She screamed for Brandon to hurry, and they sped off.

The couple drove straight to the Mineral Point police station and reported what they had seen. They were so visibly frightened that the story was taken seriously. A patrol unit was sent out to Ludden Lake. The area around the jetty was searched, but nothing was found. Whoever the man had been, there was no sign of him in the area - again.

Brandon and Jamie returned to the lake the following day - in broad daylight, of course - to gather up their fishing equipment, cooler, and other items. The only thing they couldn't find was the flashlight that Brandon had thrown at the bizarre figure.

He'd apparently decided to keep it.

One of the most overlooked creatures in the history of sinister stranger encounters is the "Spring Valley Vampire." This mysterious figure, clad all in black, has been rumored to linger in the Old Lithuanian Cemetery, just outside the small town of Spring Valley, Illinois, for many years.

Stories tell of him hiding among the tombstones, preying on local cats and dogs, and terrifying anyone who dares cross through the cemetery after dark. Even in the daylight, the graveyard can be a foreboding place, and legend tells of the torn and broken bodies of stray animals that have been found, drained of blood, near the old Massock Mausoleum. This tomb is the final resting place of the Massock brothers, once well-known butchers and businessmen in the Spring Valley area.

According to the stories, the mausoleum is the lair of the vampire, and it is there where he hides during the daylight hours, only emerging after the sun goes down. In 1967, two local teenagers broke open the tomb, vandalized it, and stole the

skull from one of the bodies inside. They were later caught and punished, but their desecration of the crypt only provided new life for the horrifying stories that had been told about the graveyard for years. New incidents and vampire sightings occurred at the cemetery for years after this happened.

The infamous Massock Brothers mausoleum in the Old Lithuanian Cemetery in Spring Valley, Illinois

In the early 1980s, the story of the Spring Valley Vampire got the attention of a man who described himself as a "hardened Vietnam veteran," and he decided to take some friends and go out and see if the stories about the monster were true. They drove out of town to the cemetery and then started toward the Massock tomb through the darkness. As they approached it, there were startled to see someone moving in the shadows. Then, a tall, thin figure, draped all in black and "radiating evil," as they described it, shambled toward them. The veteran, who had brought a handgun along on the outing, pulled out the gun and reportedly shot the creature five times at point-blank range. He later stated that the bullets had absolutely no effect on it. The figure hissed and growled and lurched towards them, sending the man and his friends fleeing from the graveyard in panic.

Word spread about the incident, and eventually, some researchers in Chicago heard the story and decided to come to Spring Valley and check out the cemetery. The group arrived one afternoon about a month after the earlier incident. Walking through the cemetery grounds in the daylight, they studied the Massock mausoleum, searching for a way to gain easy access. The door was securely locked and sealed, and a group member poked a stick into a small vent on the side of the crypt. He was startled when something "black and wormy" shot out from the hole and twisted onto the ground. Unnerved, the investigators took off running.

They eventually gathered their courage and returned to the cemetery at dusk. They brought a bottle of holy water with them and emptied it into the vent. They were startled to hear what they described as a "painful groaning" coming from inside, and the group once again fled the cemetery. This time, they did not return. They decided to leave the Spring Valley Vampire to someone else.

Since that time, there have been other reports of the cemetery's vampire. Despite this, many in the area don't take the story seriously and believe it's nothing more than the product of tall tales and overactive imaginations - but not everyone thinks that way.

According to "Joan," who did not want her last name used for reasons that will soon become obvious, the Spring Valley Vampire is very real. She knows this because she encountered the creature face-to-face one night back in 1960.

Joan was only 12-years-old at the time and was over at a friend's house one summer night. She lived close to the cemetery, and her friend's house was several blocks away. She often took a shortcut through the graveyard when she was walking home. This is exactly what she did on this particular night, but she was coming home much later than usual this time. Darkness had already fallen, and she knew that she would likely get in trouble with her mother for getting home so later. She later recalled that this was the only thing on her mind that night as she hurried through the cemetery.

Joan walked quickly among the tombstones, pondering what excuse she would give her mother when she arrived at home when suddenly, she was knocked to the ground.

In an interview that she gave more than 45 years after the incident, she told of how she was hit very hard in the back and shoved down onto the ground. She had not heard anyone approaching her and had seen no one else in the cemetery. When her eyes focused, though, she saw a figure standing over her that was exceedingly tall and gaunt. The figure bent down towards her from the waist, and she saw that it was a man with a set of very long, yellow, and sharp teeth. The experience, she said, was so "surreal and unsettling" that she is unable to remember what happened next. All she knows is that the figure was there one moment and then gone the next. She couldn't even remember how she got home that night, what her mother said to her, or going to bed.

However, she did recall waking up the next morning, getting dressed, and going back to the cemetery to look for some evidence that the strange incident had actually taken place. It had rained the day before, and the ground had been soft, so it was easy for her to find her footprints in the wet soil. She could see where she entered the graveyard, where the ground was disturbed when she had been pushed down, but nothing else. The other person, whoever he had been, had left no footprints behind.

What, or who was it that Joan encountered that night in 1960? Was it the vampire, or at least a mysterious figure of some sort, that lurked in the Spring Valley cemetery? No one can say, but she maintains that the incident really occurred even after all these years.

"What I can tell you are the things that happened to me," she said. "I know they are true."

4. ATTACK OF THE

KILLER CLOWNS

"There's nothing funny about a clown in the moonlight." – Lon Chaney

The man who came to Hamelin certainly got the attention of the people who hired him to come there and repel the invaders that had taken over the town. The man's clothing was brightly colored, almost garish, resembling that of a jester who entertained at fairs. It made the adults take a second glance at the unusual man, but the children, well, the children were entranced.

Hamelin, an old German town even in the late 1200s, was under a state of siege when this story took place. The siege was not by an army of hostile soldiers but by rats - thousands of them. The people of the town had no way to bring the infestation to an end until the mysterious and oddly dressed stranger arrived in town.

He claimed to know how to get rid of

the rats, and he wouldn't use weapons or poison. The only thing he had with him was a musical instrument. And hence, the legend of the Pied Piper begins.

Using his pipe, the colorfully dressed man - "pied" means "decorated, by the way - created an enchanting and hypnotic tune that lured the entire rat population into waters of the nearby river, drowning each and every one of them. All that he asked in return was a payment of 1,000 guilders - "golden pennies" - and the mayor of Hamelin eagerly agreed to the payment. Then, for whatever reason, he refused to pay the Piper. He accused the Piper of bringing the rats to Hamelin in the first place so that he could lure them away and claim a reward.

Whether the accusation was true or not, the Piper promised the town had not seen the last of him. He warned the mayor that terrible things would befall the town if he didn't pay him what he was owed.

It was not an idle threat.

According to written accounts, the Piper returned to Hamelin on June 26, 1284, a day that celebrated the lives of the saints, John and Paul. It was also on that day that 130 of the town's children mysteriously vanished.

The Piper had walked into town, pulled out his pipe, and began playing the same tune that had entranced the town's rat populations. Children poured from their homes and playgrounds and followed the Piper as he led them out of town.

Only three children remained in Hamelin after the Piper's final visit - one was deaf, another disabled, and the third was blind. He had tried to follow the other children but had lost his way. The rest of the town's children were gone - and never seen again.

Over the years, some have dismissed this story as folklore, a tale to terrify young children. However, the written records state that it actually happened, so it's likely some version of it did.

Some say that the children all died from a plague brought on by the rats that infested the town. Others say that the story grew out of the so-called Children's Crusade of a few decades earlier when 20,000 youth of France and Germany marched off the Holy Land to liberate Jerusalem and were never seen again.

Whatever its origin, the tale is well-known and has been told and re-told many times, including in a very famous poem by Robert Browning. The town of Hamelin certainly exists, and perhaps the Pied Piper once did, too.

And if so, then he stands today as the original "killer clown," a sinister figure in garish makeup and extravagant clothing who lures children to their doom. The Pied Piper may have been the first, but he was certainly not the last.

CONFEDERATE GHOSTS AND "NIGHT DOCTORS"

There have been attacks by sinister strangers in America since at least 1692 when mysterious soldiers menaced settlers in Massachusetts (see next chapter). You'll find many of the gassers, leapers, bunny men, barbers, and phantoms within the pages of this book. And yet the stories of clowns menacing children are a recent phenomenon. Even so, they seem to have roots deep in our collective past.

America's first costumed creeps, who were apt to carry off both children and adults, emerged after the Civil War when the Confederacy was beaten into submission by United States' forces. The practice of slavery in this country -- which began when the first Africans were brought to these shores in chains in 1619 -- ended with the war. When formerly enslaved people began to gain political power under the protection of occupying federal troops, many southern whites began a campaign to try and restore the old system. Many groups were assembled to try and drive out the northern carpetbaggers, including paramilitary groups like the White League, Redcaps, Knights of the White Camellia, and, most importantly, the Ku Klux Klan.

The racist idiocy of the Ku Klux Klan began as a "fraternal order" that was designed to frighten black families by claiming to be the ghosts of slain Confederate soldiers who would carry away their children.

The Klan began as a fraternal order started by Confederate veterans in 1865, with extravagant titles, ceremonies, and all the earmarks of secret societies like the Freemasons. But that would soon change. The group soon began a campaign of violence and intimidation, aimed almost entirely at African Americans.

As the focal point of this campaign, they used the supernatural to try and frighten poor, uneducated people, pretending to be the ghosts of slain Confederate soldiers.

The white robes and pointed hoods came later, though. The early Klansmen rose on horseback wearing strange masks, fake beards, horns, and peaked hats. They visited black families to play cruel tricks on them, such as demanding a drink and seeming to swallow buckets of water that they were emptying into a rubber bag. They sometimes extended skeletal hands to shake or pretended to remove their own heads using paper replicas.

It was stupid and childish and seemed like something out of the circus, clowns and all. But these clowns were dangerous. Along with the Klan's "pranks," homes were burned, people were shot, lynched, and beaten. It was said that some of the unfortunates who crossed their path were never seen again.

And if the Klan wasn't bad enough, there were the "Night Doctors."

The Night Doctors came to life in African American folklore during this same period after the Civil War. The stories were initially spread by former enslavers who wanted to make the formerly enslaved people too afraid to leave the plantations after they were set free.

Legend has it that the Night Doctors were doctors, medical students, and corpse buyers who went out after dark, looking for victims.

The Night Doctors were said to wear masks, hoods, and white coats. They rode the highways and back roads at night, abducting African Americans so they could perform experiments on them. The doctors, it was claimed, used chloroform to subdue their victims and put adhesive plaster over their mouths to stifle their cries. Once captured, they were bound, gagged, and blindfolded and put into a black wagon with rubber wheels that made no sound as the prisoners were quietly wheeled off to a medical facility to be dissected, tortured, and killed so their organs could be harvested.

Or so the stories claimed. True or not, they worked - many people stayed behind locked doors at night and off the roads, terrified that the Night Doctors would find them.

While the "night doctors" of African American legend – white men who carried away black children to conduct terrible experiments on them – were a folktale, the story had a basis in the truth.

The stories may seem silly today, but tragically, stories of white doctors victimizing black people have taken root from some pretty horrific truths.

During the early nineteenth century, medical students often had to resort to grave robbing to procure cadavers to practice their surgical skills. In many states during the nineteenth century, it was illegal for students to dissect human corpses - well, white human corpses anyway. There were no such restrictions on the bodies of African Americans.

Poor, disenfranchised blacks were nearly powerless to protect their dead. To make matters worse, doctors and medical students also performed surgeries on living candidates - all of them black. Southern teaching hospitals would only perform live surgeries for medical students on African Americans.

Later, it would get even worse. In 1932, Alabama's Public Health Service and Tuskegee University launched the Tuskegee Syphilis Study. They took 600 African American men - 399 of them who already had syphilis and 201 that did not - and promised them food, free medical care, and burial insurance if they consented to be treated with radical new techniques.

During the study, investigators wanted to observe the progression of the disease but only told the participants they were being treated for "bad blood." They never told them they had syphilis or that a new treatment by penicillin was available. They didn't give them anything. The Tuskegee scientists wanted to see what happened to the men with no medicine or knowledge about their illness.

The study - now known as the most infamous medical study in American history - continued until 1972, when the plug was finally pulled after a leak to the press. Numerous participants died of syphilis. Forty of their wives contracted the disease, and 19 children were born with congenital disabilities because of it.

THE 1981 CLOWN SIGHTINGS

Obviously, "killer clowns" did not step out of the collective imagination of America fully formed. Like the Klan or the "Night Doctors," they were a traditional terror that changed to cope with a contemporary threat.

But why clowns? Aren't they supposed to be wacky, entertaining characters from the circus, designed to make us laugh? They are, but honestly, I don't know many people who think clowns are funny - especially when they're trying to pull children into vans or are standing on a dark street at night, holding a handful of balloons.

Coulrophobia - a fear of clowns - is real, and it's no laughing matter. It's rare for a genuine phobia, but many people find clowns creepy and even downright scary. And there may be a psychological reason for it.

For starters, a clown's makeup can be unsettling. It hides not only the person's identity but also that person's feelings. A

clown has a
painted-on
smile, and we
are quick to
believe they
have
something to
hide. Then,
there's the
disturbing
nature of the
makeup itself.
The oversized
lips and
eyebrows
distort the
face so that
our brain
perceives
them as
having a
human face,
but there's
something wrong with it. That oddness is heightened by a
clown's bizarre costume. In addition, clowns are unpredictable
by nature, which puts people on edge.

These psychological discomforts produce a fear that is then
stoked by negative portrayals of clowns in popular culture like
horror films and books -especially when associated with one of
the most depraved serial killers in American history.

John Wayne Gacy was believed to be a respectable
Chicago contractor. He was married, was a Jaycees "Man of
the Year" who participated in local politics, and entertained at

charity events dressed as a clown. But in December 1978, it was learned that this upstanding businessman had raped, tortured, and murdered more than 33 young men and boys and had buried most of their bodies under his suburban ranch house.

Gacy is an obvious inspiration for many people's fear of clowns. He was dubbed a "killer clown" by the press, and his murders were covered extensively in the national news. He was a sexual sadist, and many of his victims were minors. Like the Pied Piper, he lured away the children, and they were never seen again.

There is no question that Gacy - along with horrific portrayals of clowns in fiction and films - has influenced not only our fears but many of the sightings of sinister clowns, too. American outbreaks of clown "attacks" almost always seem to coincide with something happening in the news or popular culture - and in just about every case, it's something terrible.

But let's go back to 1981, to the first "killer clowns" reported, and follow the trail up to the present day.

In the spring of that year, strange stories began to emerge from the area around Boston, Massachusetts. It seems that several individuals in multicolored clothing, driving panel vans, were trying to lure children away with them. Soon, the stories of clowns in vans bothering children were being spread by newspapers, schools, local police, and dozens of parents.

At that time, researcher Loren Coleman lived in Cambridge, Massachusetts, and heard about the first reports of clowns trying to lure kids into their vans. As more and more of these reports came in from surrounding towns, he knew that something odd was happening. He wrote to many of his contacts - there was no email or quick online method of reaching anyone in those days - and was startled to discover that clown reports were occurring all over the United States. Stranger still, most of them were being ignored by the media because it was all --

well, just too weird. It would be Loren who single-handedly chronicled the clown attacks of 1981.

On May 6, the Boston police began receiving numerous complaints about men in clown suits harassing elementary school children. One man was seen wearing clown makeup and half of a clown suit - he was naked from the waist down. He was seen driving a black van in Franklin Park in Roxbury. He was also spotted at the Mary E. Curley School in the Jamaica Plain neighborhood.

A day earlier, in Brookline, two men wearing clown outfits had tried to lure children into their van by offering them candy. The van was an older model, black, with ladders on the side, a broken headlight, and no hub caps - so, not exactly forgettable. After the van was seen near the Lawrence Elementary School, the police told school administrators to be "extra cautious." School Superintendent Robert Sperber contacted all ten elementary school principals in the district and asked them to warn the students.

According to a memo that was sent out, "It has been brought to the attention of the police department and the district office that adults dressed as clowns have been bothering children to and from the school. Please advise all students that they must stay away from strangers, especially ones dressed as clowns."

This seems to be good advice under any circumstances, but the warnings managed to increase the panic that was already brewing because of the incidents.

By May 8, reports of clowns were pouring in. Accounts of clowns giving candy to children in schoolyards and trying to entice them into vans were flooding into police precincts, and officers were frantically trying to find the offenders. They were stopping vans and pickups and legitimate clowns delivering flowers and birthday greetings. Thankfully, the circus was not in town. Regardless, no pedophiles in clown costumes were arrested.

So, as often happens when the police can't get to the bottom of strange events, frustrated officials began discounting the reports. They claimed that virtually all the reported sightings had originated with children between five and seven years old. This wasn't true, but it made it easy to dismiss reports from children that young. They said there was no solid evidence of any children being harassed, injured, molested, or kidnapped by clowns.

"If it's someone's idea of a joke, it's a sick joke," Cambridge Police Captain Alan Hughes told reporters. "We had rumors, but nothing substantiated. No adult or police officer has even seen a clown. We've had calls saying there was a clown at a certain intersection, and we happened to have cars sitting there, and the officers saw nothing. We've had over 20 calls on 911. When the officers get there, no one tells them anything. I don't know if someone's got a hoax going or not, but it's really foolhardy."

As we have seen with many past incidents like this - especially the "Black Ghost" sightings - it's very possible that a handful of sightings turned into a hysteria that caused witnesses to mistake ordinary clowns for threatening ones, but dismissing the events entirely is more "foolhardy" than a "hoax" that would have required multiple actors and complicated logistics.

It didn't matter, though. Newspaper stories that showed the frustration of the cops managed to calm down the public, and the story died out.

Well, in Boston anyway.

Almost immediately, reports of clowns disturbing children began in Providence, Rhode Island, about 50 miles to the south. These stories were being reported by social workers, who were, in turn, hearing it from the children they were counseling. Those stories could have been urban legends or even spillover from the reports in Boston, but the next ones were much harder to dismiss.

The clowns - certainly different ones, but still clowns - traveled about 1,000 miles west to both Kansas City, Kansas, and Kansas City, Missouri.

On May 18, the police began receiving telephone calls from parents telling them that their children had been threatened and harassed by a man in a clown costume and makeup.

Lieutenant Michael Dailey stated, "We are going on the assumption that he exists, but we believe some of the reports are exaggerated by a panic-type atmosphere. We're not saying he isn't out there, but so far, not one adult has reported any sighting."

That would soon change, but, for now, it was children who had seen the man. The clown was described as having a white-painted face and wearing a costume with a picture of the Devil on the front. He was reportedly driving a van - described variously as yellow, orange, or red - that had candy canes and spiders painted on the sides.

Most of the initial calls to the police and school administrators came from the Fairfax, Hawthorne, Banneker, and Grant elementary school neighborhoods. But as things escalated, they also started receiving calls from the Parker, Haskell, Pearson, and Welborn school areas.

Carol Rush, who had two daughters at Fairfax Elementary, explained to reporters that her girls told her about a man in a clown suit who was on school grounds, bothering the children, but that she didn't pay much attention to the story until a friend telephoned her. The friend said that her daughter came home crying and told a similar story. In her case, a clown had come to the window of the Hawthorne school, scaring and chasing the children.

As rumors spread around the city, the menacing character was given the moniker of the "Killer Clown," even though at this point, there had been no substantiated accounts of him attacking or threatening anyone. All the reports of the clown had come from children, which made the police skeptical.

But that changed on May 22. By that afternoon, police cars were scouring the city for a yellow van that was being driven by a clown who had tried to abduct two children earlier that day.

At 8:30 a.m., a woman watched as her six and 7-year-old daughters walked to their bus stop. Before they could reach it, a yellow van pulled up to them, and someone inside it spoke to the two girls. Whatever was said, they screamed and immediately turned and ran back home. The yellow van sped away.

The girls told their mother that a clown with a knife had ordered them to get into his van. The woman drove her children to school and reported the incident less than an hour later.

By then, the police had already received dozens of reports of a clown in a yellow van. The first order to pick up anyone matching the clown's description went out to police officers by 11:00 a.m. Radio stations that monitored the police band started broadcasting the manhunt a short time later.

But this didn't stop the "Killer Clown."

Around 3:00 p.m., just as elementary schools were starting to dismiss for the day, calls about a clown trying to lure children into a yellow van began pouring in to police dispatchers. The reports came from six different elementary schools, and police cars crisscrossed the city, trying to track down the elusive clown.

The calls lasted for the next two hours and then finally tapered off. In every case, children claimed that a clown had chased them home, looked at them through their windows, or had tried to threaten them into getting into his van.

But the sheer number of calls was not enough to convince the police that they were chasing a flesh and blood monster. The woman who reported the yellow van seemed credible, but what if it was an isolated incident, or worse, a copycat pretending to be the fake "Killer Clown"?

The police and some mental health professionals in the area decided to dismiss the whole thing as hysteria. The clown sightings had simply not been verified, school officials said. "But those kids were terrified," Hawthorne Principal Wendell Edwards said. "They were upset all day." But as far as the authorities were concerned, they were frightened by nothing more than an urban legend.

Maybe. But there were still eyewitness accounts coming in after the police began calling the whole thing a hoax. A sixth-grader named LaTanya Johnson saw the clown near the Fairfax Elementary School. "He was by the fence and ran down through the big yard when some kids ran over there. He ran toward a yellow van. He was dressed in a black shirt with a devil on the front. He had two candy canes down each side of his pants. The pants were black, too, I think. I don't remember much about his face."

But it wouldn't matter. The police had dismissed the whole thing, and the sightings stopped a short time later.

Why? Maybe because the clown - or clowns - moved on to Omaha and Denver, where incidents involving children being harassed by clowns were also reported.

In June 1981, clowns were up to no good in Pittsburgh. Well, not just clowns - apparently, there was a gorilla, a giant bunny rabbit, and Spider-Man harassing kids, too.

The first report appeared in the newspaper as occurring on June 2. The police had received reports from two of the city's housing projects - Arlington Heights and Garfield - that "someone dressed in a mask" was scaring children. Sergeant

Charles Schweinberg said that calls had started coming in the previous weekend. "The children are obviously frightened, but fortunately, we have not had a report of anyone being molested or even touched."

On June 3, children in the Hill District in Pittsburgh claimed that two clowns in a van had been bothering them.

And then back to the Garfield neighborhood, where someone wearing a pink and white rabbit costume frightened a group of children and then hopped away to a blue van. Three boys who reported the rabbit insisted that it was real, but they didn't want their names in the paper. As one said, "We're afraid the rabbit will track us down and kill us."

Before long, the police were receiving as many as 15 calls each day - mostly from the city's housing projects - about children being harassed by clowns, a man in a gorilla suit, and a man in a Spider-Man costume. One report claimed that all three showed up in the Arlington Heights project and tried to get a young boy into their van.

After a clown was spotted in Terrace Village, the police conducted a search with the assistance of two canine patrols and 100 local kids, most carrying clubs and baseball bats. They didn't find any clowns, but witnesses insisted the costumed man had been real.

As in the other cities, the sightings simply stopped. Was it group hysteria or simply spreading an urban legend to six large American cities?

As I mentioned earlier, many sightings coincided with things happening in the news or in pop culture. If we look at it this way, the incidents in Pittsburgh's housing projects are the easiest to understand.

At the same time costumed characters and clowns were threatening African American children in the Pittsburgh housing projects, a serial killer was stalking the streets of Atlanta and making national news. Between July 1979 and June 1981, dozens of black children were murdered. Almost all the victims were male, and many were strangled or suffocated, and their bodies were hidden in overgrown areas. Over time, the pattern changed and began to include adult men, too, whose bodies were sometimes dropped into local rivers. Witnesses to a loud splash coming from the Chattahoochee River led the police to Wayne Williams, who was eventually convicted and sent to prison for his crimes.

Tension was high in black communities at the time, especially when it turned out that the killer was also black. It had been assumed - including by the police - that the murders were being committed by white racists, which had ratcheted up fear in many places.

If black children were being raped and murdered in Atlanta by an unknown killer, why not a clown or men in gorilla and rabbit suits in Pittsburgh. Perhaps like in other incidents of this kind, one clown or one rabbit was seen, and the story spread, changed, grew, and spun out of control.

Other explanations for the plethora of clown sightings in 1981 have also been offered. Many have blamed Stephen King. They say that his book, *It*, about a terrifying clown that takes children into a sewer, is to blame for the 1981 incidents. I will agree that Stephen King has done a lot to scare people into being horrified by clowns, but *It* wasn't even published until 1986, five years after the events occurred.

We'll never know what happened for sure, but I think we can all agree that something very weird was happening in 1981 with clowns.

ATTACK OF THE CLOWNS CONTINUES

And the sightings of sinister clowns didn't stop there. Reports of clowns in vans and creeping along streets or in alleys and parks continued. There were more sightings in Boston in 1983, in Phoenix in 1985, in Newark in 1991, and in Washington, D.C. and Capitol Heights, Maryland, in 1994.

In March 1988, children across a three-county area near Louisville, Kentucky, began calling the police to report a malevolent clown who was offering rides in a red pickup truck. In one case, the clown even pursued one of the children on foot. No arrests were made, and the clown disappeared without a trace.

In October 1991, more than 40 children - and some of their parents - in Erie, Pennsylvania, reported a clown prowling around neighborhood backyards and peeping in windows. He was never caught.

That same month, police in Chicago began receiving reports of a man dressed as "Homey the Clown" from the television show, *In Living Color*. He was attempting to lure children into his van with offers of candy and money. As in most other cases, the reports came mainly from children, but the authorities insisted they were "taking the sightings seriously," especially since they were coming in from all over the city.

This clown was described as African American, about five-foot-11-inches tall, and reportedly seen driving a red, white, or blue van with the words "Ha-Ha" painted on the side. Other reports identified his vehicle as a black pickup truck and a black Oldsmobile. Police speculated that there could be more than one "evil Homey" loose in the city.

Elementary schools sent home letters to parents as the reports of sightings reached a fever pitch on October 10. Sharon Adelman Reyes, principal of Longfellow Elementary in Oak Park, stated, "We want to take every precaution, but at the same time, we don't want to unnecessarily panic people. I think it's a rumor that is getting out of hand."

A woman whose grandchild attended Lemoyne School in Chicago told reporters that school officials had stepped up patrols and that her 10-year-old grandson told her that he had seen the clown crossing the street. He also claimed that other students had seen someone dressed as a clown looking into the library windows.

Casper Hearon, an eighth-grader from Nettlehorst School, told the *Tribune* that many children were afraid to walk home after dark since the clown sightings had started. "I heard there's not just one, there's 10 of them," he said.

Sherman G. Chambers, assistant principal at Reavis School, said that an eighth grader had told him that he and his sister had been confronted by a clown wearing a red wig, large red nose, yellow costume, and red shoes earlier the previous week. According to the boy, he had punched him in the nose, and the clown had fled.

Chambers told a reporter, "I kinda believe this had to be true. This is a big eighth-grader who told me."

Somehow, both Chambers and the reporter missed the fact that this is an exact description of the famous fast-food clown, Ronald McDonald. When we add "Homey" to the mix, we have another example of popular culture influencing a figure dressing as a clown - and possibly influencing those who claim to see the figure, too.

And that's likely not the only effect pop culture had on clown sightings and attacks in the early 1990s. The other was the release of the popular television mini-series adaptation of Stephen King's book, *It*. It's hard for us to imagine in these days of streaming services and endless entertainment what it was like when a new mini-series aired on television at that time. It was "must-watch TV," and it was incredibly successful when it aired in two parts in November 1990, garnering nearly 30 million viewers. During a time when recording television programs on tape with a VCR was becoming a common practice in family homes, the second part of *It* was the most taped program of the month of November.

And then there was "Pennywise," the clown, portrayed by Tim Curry. Ask anyone who remembers his version of the character, and they can assure you that it was nightmare fuel. Over the years, I have met many people who tell me that their fear of clowns is directly connected to Tim Curry and "Pennywise."

Is it any wonder that clown sightings made a comeback around this same time?

But we can't blame all clown sightings on Stephen King and Tim Curry - although Mr. King will be taking another hit before this chapter is finished.

Multiple reports of an "evil clown" were received by the police in Galveston, Texas, in October 1992. The first report came from the parents of a small girl who said that a clown tried to abduct her. Soon, more reports came in, always from areas around elementary schools, but despite the authorities' best efforts, the clown was never captured.

In June 1994, multiple reports were received by police in Washington, D.C.'s Seventh District about a clown who was trying to lure children into his van. The police didn't bother to investigate. By November, their lack of attention to this case - as well as the disappearance of a young boy - was used by local activists as examples of the police ignoring or disbelieving crimes reported by African Americans.

Six clown incidents occurred in South Brunswick and Howell, New Jersey, in August 1997. Local children began reporting a clown leaping out at them from behind trees outside local housing projects and laughing maniacally. The police increased patrols in the areas but claimed the sightings - of the same clown - are "unrelated."

On June 19, 2000, a man dressed as a clown and holding balloons tried to lure children into the woods near Fitchburg's King James Court Apartments.

The children, who ranged in age between 6 and 10, were at the apartment complex's playground when the clown appeared in the woods nearby and asked them to come and talk to him. When the children refused and began to walk away, the man again asked them to come into the woods.

The children then ran home and told their parents about the clown. The adults returned to the scene, and while they could not find the clown, one of them saw a balloon floating off into the sky.

The police investigated and even brought in a dog to try and track the man, but they were unable to find him. A bulletin was put out with the man's description, stating that he was between five-foot-six and five-foot-ten and medium build. He was wearing a white wig, a red nose, giant red shoes, yellow overalls, and, strangely, black face paint.

Whoever he was, he was never found.

In October 2008, Chicago's Wicker Park neighborhood was the site of an attempted abduction by a sinister clown, who tried to use balloons to lure a child into his van. More sightings occurred on the city's South Side soon after, with the man's description and methods identical to the earlier ones. The man wore a wig and white face paint with teardrops on one cheek. In each report, he approached the children as they walked to and from school and was driving a white or light brown van with a window broken out.

On October 12, the clown was seen on foot in the Garfield Park neighborhood near Beidler Elementary School and the Polaris Charter Academy. He was dressed in a multi-colored costume, white face paint, and the distinctive teardrops on one cheek. After a failed attempt to abduct a child, he escaped in a van.

The police could never collect any hard evidence leading to the man's arrest, and after the October 12 attempted abduction, the sightings stopped.

In October 2014, the town of Wasco, California, was terrorized by a group of clowns that appeared on the streets at night carrying party props like balloons and horns, as well as more menacing objects like knives, baseball bats, and machetes. On one occasion, a witness reported a clown slowly rocking back and forth on a mechanical unicorn by the side of a deserted street. How's that for creepy?

Nearly 20 reports of clowns came into police during the first week of sightings, but the authorities were unable to discover who was behind the incidents. They didn't know if it was one person, or an entire gang of them - or even if they could do anything about it. None of the clowns were connected to any crimes. However, one Kern County Sheriff's deputy did say there had been eyewitness reports of the clowns engaging in criminal behavior, and one young boy had been allegedly chased down the street by a clown wielding an ax.

Making the situation even stranger was a social media account that had appeared from someone who called themselves "Wasco the Clown." He claimed responsibility for many of the sightings. He repeatedly posted sinister messages, such as: "I am the creepy, evil-looking clown that is roaming the streets of Wasco, California at night. Come Find Me. I will give you a balloon."

Police in Bakersfield eventually arrested a 14-year-old dressed as a clown, reportedly chasing people around at night, but when he was questioned, the boy said that he was just playing a prank and copying the online clown.

As if to prove that police had the wrong suspect, social media posts became more active from the ominous "Wasco." Photos of clowns posing in various places in Wasco, Delano, and Bakersfield began appearing, along with captions like "come out and play" and "It's funny you guys think I got arrested." In many of the images there was more than one clown, and they were often in threatening poses or brandishing weapons.

One of the many eerie photos that were posted on social media by "Wasco the Clown."

The clowns - and their social media presence - became so notorious that they became celebrities of sorts and people drove around at night, hoping to spot them. Speculation about the clowns theorized that they were Halloween pranksters or some kind of cult, but no one really knew.

The investigation into the clown sightings went nowhere, and no further arrests were ever made. Wasco continued to be inundated with clown sightings, and soon, the phenomenon spread out through the entire San Joaquin Valley, with police estimating there were at least 20 clowns in the area at one point.

But no arrests were made, no evidence was found, and there were no leads to follow. In time, the sightings faded, and the story went cold. You can still find social media references to

"Wasco the Clown," but there have been no new posts since 2014.

Whoever "Wasco" and the others were, they have vanished into the place where old social media accounts go to die.

As the Wasco, California sightings were heating up, theories about the clowns were coming from all directions. In addition to pranks or a cult, some suggested that the clowns were a publicity stunt for an upcoming horror film. They weren't, but a flurry of other clown sightings in 2014 were linked to a movie.

In March 2014, a film production company took responsibility for a clown scare on Staten Island, New York, where images of a creepy-looking clown carrying balloons and stalking neighborhoods after dark started appearing on social media. The clown wore a yellow costume, a white puffy collar, and a trademark red nose.

But other sightings continued.

In July 2015, a clown was spotted in Chicago's Rosehill Cemetery. He was seen by two witnesses scaling a fence and entering the cemetery late at night. Realizing that he had an audience, the clown turned and waved at them and then ran off into a dark wooded area and was not seen again. Police investigation of the sighting did not lead to any arrests.

And then came the "clown mania" of 2016.

Once again, Stephen King would be blamed for the rash of terrifying sightings of clowns that occurred in a dozen different states that fall. Publicity had recently started for the film adaptation of his book, *It*, and while audiences knew little of what would be in the finished film - released a year *after* these sightings in September 2017, by the way - they knew the terrifying "Pennywise" would be back. But can we really blame *It* again? There's no question that *It* had become a permanent part of American pop culture by 2016, but whether it influenced what happened a year before the new film premiered in theaters is anyone's guess.

The 2016 clown sightings began in August in Greenville, South Carolina. The stories, once again, began with children telling adults that a group of clowns had tried to lure them into the woods. But the stories took an even darker turn when adults began encountering them, too. Reports were filed with the police about people in clown makeup terrorizing adults and children alike at an apartment complex.

Soon after, a woman who was walking home late at night reported that she saw a "large-figured" clown waving at her from under a streetlight. She waved back.

Another woman reported to the police that her son heard clanging chains and a banging noise at his front door. He looked out and saw a clown outside.

The police were unsure whether the stories were coming from children's imagination or something sinister was afoot. They did confirm that some of the apartment complex residents had fired shots into the woods at the fleeing clowns. They were unable to confirm the actual sightings, though, but did add extra deputies to patrol the area and helped distribute flyers that warned children about walking in the woods alone at night.

Clown panic swept the city, and calls to the police continued in the days that followed, including a call from the parents of another child at a different apartment complex who had also been harassed by a clown.

As the incidents in Greenville began drawing national publicity, calls to the police about clowns spread rapidly through the Carolinas and then on to the rest of the nation. The fear spread, sometimes perpetuated by the authorities themselves but largely by the media, which was starting to report clown sightings and attempted abductions seriously for the first time.

Clown sightings occurred throughout Florida, Georgia, Arkansas, Mississippi, Missouri, Louisiana, Texas, Virginia, West Virginia, Maryland, Delaware, New Jersey, Massachusetts, Rhode Island, Pennsylvania, Ohio, Indiana, Michigan, Minnesota, Illinois, Iowa, Nebraska, Kansas, Colorado, Utah, Idaho, Oregon, and Washington. By the end of the month, the *New York Times* called the clown incidents "a contagion." Almost every night on the national news, new sightings were being reported somewhere.

In Concord, California, a woman told police that a man in a clown suit had attempted to kidnap her infant daughter while she was seated at a bus stop.

In New York City, a man named Ioannis Markesinis reported seeing a shadowy figure standing under a streetlight outside of his home. The figure had a stark white face, red curly hair, a red nose, and a jumpsuit. He gestured at Ioannis to come outside - with a knife in his hand.

More reports came in from the city, including from the 96th Street station of the 6 train, where a clown reportedly scared the daylights out of a 16-year-old stepping off a northbound train at 2:00 in the afternoon.

The clown mania spread to schools. Online clowns threatened the lives of children and led to the lockdown of two high schools in Queens and two on Long Island during the week of September 25.

That same week, a 14-year-old girl was arrested for calling in a threat to a Washington, D.C. middle school, claiming that clowns were coming to the school with weapons.

In New Haven, Connecticut, school officials banned clown costumes after several menacing clown-related social media posts were made against schools in the district. An armed clown hoax temporarily put a Massachusetts college on lockdown.

Then on October 3, hundreds of students at Pennsylvania State University swarmed surrounding campus streets to carry out a mass clown hunt after reports circulated that a clown was harassing female students.

The sightings continued into October and only dropped off after a promised "clown purge" - yes, like the popular *Purge* films with clowns imitating pop culture again -- that was supposed to take place on Halloween never happened.

It made for a disconcerting autumn for many people in 2016, but just as it had done in the past, the incidents came to an end with no solution.

What do we make of the "killer clowns" who have haunted America's recent history? Are they real, or merely hoaxes spun from our urban legends and imaginations?

I think that it's obvious that the incidents go hand-in-hand with what's happening in the news and in our culture at the time of multiple attacks. In the early 1980s, they co-existed alongside the "Satanic Panic" period, when cults were allegedly kidnapping children all over the country for their rituals. In the early 1990s, there were the Atlanta child murders. In between, you had John Wayne Gacy, Stephen King's *It*, and more.

Clown sightings are obviously common during times of social uncertainty - as evidenced by what was just listed and also by the rising tensions caused by the elections of 2016.

So, are these clowns real, fake, or somewhere in the middle? I'm not sure that I can answer that question. I'm not sure that any of us can. It's possible that the clown sightings in this chapter started as one thing and became another - or perhaps just as eerily, they are something that we conjured up all on our own.

5. THE SINISTER STRANGERS

On the evening of August 21, 1955, five adults and seven children came into the Hopkinsville, Kentucky, police station with a very strange story. They claimed that a farmhouse where they had been staying the night was attacked by "little green men."

Billy Ray Taylor, who had been staying with the Sutton family at the house, was the first witness to the unusual events. He had gone out to fetch some water from the well but came running back into the house moments later, yelling that he had seen something that might have been a "flying saucer" land in a gulley near the house.

The Suttons laughed at him - but not for long. An hour later, the frenzied barking of their dogs alerted them to the presence of a "glowing goblin" approaching the house. The Suttons then did what any self-respecting Kentucky hill family would do when confronted with a threat - they ran out into the yard with shotguns and pistols and opened fire. John Sutton stated that one of his bullets struck the creature, and it did a backflip and ran away.

The "goblin" soon returned - and he brought a friend. They began peering into the windows, terrifying the adults and children barricaded inside the house. The creatures had large, domed heads with two short antennae, pointed chins, large, pointed ears, bulging yellow eyes, thick noses, no lips to speak of, and no necks. They were approximately three feet tall, and their spindly arms and legs were contradicted by powerful chests. Their arms were nearly twice as long as their legs, and their feet were like suction cups. At one point, when Billy Ray came outside to look for the creatures, one of the goblins reached down with four-clawed, webbed fingers and grabbed a handful of his hair.

John and Billy Ray claimed to have fought off the little men for hours, watching them flip and float, but never die after being shot. Finally, the frightened group piled into their cars and fled to the Hopkinsville police station, seven miles away. Chief Russell Greenwell, not knowing what to make of their story, but recognizing their genuine terror, gathered some deputies and went out to the farm to investigate.

When they arrived at the Sutton farm, they saw no sign of the creatures. There were no tracks or markings outside of the home, only the evidence of gunshots fired from inside. Another officer reported seeing a meteor shower in the area but no flying saucer. According to the Suttons, though, once the police left, the goblins returned and continued to look in the windows until near sunrise. After that, they vanished.

The news quickly spread of the "Hopkinsville Goblins" and reporting about the incident helped popularize the term "little green men" as a nickname for aliens, even though the group never described the creatures as green. The story spreads like wildfire among researchers of the strange.

But, of course, not everyone believed the attackers were real, even though investigations by the police, reporters, Air Force officers, and civilian researchers found no evidence of a hoax. Initially, some skeptics claimed the witnesses were drunk, but Chief Greenwell testified that they were not. The chief also later added that it was evident something "beyond reason, not ordinary" had happened to Billy Ray and the Suttons.

Since then - with the luxury of hindsight - alternative explanations have emerged, like the idea the creatures were test flight monkeys used in rocket experiments that had crashed in the area. Others refuse to consider that it was anything other than a hoax, or perhaps, more charitably, that the group, shocked by the meteor shower and in a state of panic and likely intoxicated, confused a pair of aggressive Great Horned Owls with a group of sinister strangers out to do them harm.

I think it's safe to say that this incident remains eerily unsolved.

This book has been filled with "sinister strangers," and although the Hopkinsville Goblins are probably the only ones that may have come from outer space, who knows? But I think that you'll find that most of the weird figures included here are homegrown, right here in America.

They have been with us for centuries, poking, prodding, stalking, lurking, threatening, and attacking us since colonial times. They come and go without warning and sometimes return to wreak havoc again and again.

They have certainly left their mark on our history, no matter who or what they may be.

PHANTOMS IN THE PINES

In 1692 - the same year that the people of Salem were losing their collective minds over witchcraft - a different kind of havoc was being wreaked in the seaport of Gloucester, Massachusetts, just 15 miles away.

When the first mysterious figures appeared in the woods around the community, it was assumed they were part of a French or Native American raiding party, which was not unexpected. England was at war with France, which had led to frequent attacks on the more isolated colonial settlements by French soldiers and their Iroquois allies. As recently as October 1691, raiders had murdered families along the Merrimack River, not far away from Gloucester. So, when the strange men began to be seen in the surrounding woods, the villagers armed themselves and took refuge in the garrison.

This was the sensible response to something that turned out to be beyond the senses of anything the people of Gloucester were prepared for.

The attackers boldly advanced on the village, and for two weeks, there were alarms, ambushes, and pursuits. Still, the mysterious raiders seemed immune to the effects of the settler's muskets - and apparently, to the laws of gravity and perhaps even those of time and space. They appeared without explanation and vanished just as easily, leaving nothing behind but a single bullet that was lodged in a hemlock tree and a scattering of footprints.

These sinister strangers were like nothing America had seen before - and nothing like anything we have seen since.

The village of Gloucester was founded on Cape Ann in 1623, just three years after the Pilgrims landed at Plymouth. It was the first seaport on the east coast and eventually became an important center for fishing and shipbuilding. Before it gained prominence, though, it was a simple community of rugged colonists who worked hard for their existence. Their simple way of life is perhaps what made the encounters with the phantom attackers even more disconcerting.

The strangers first appeared in a remote area east of Gloucester and near present-day Rockport and Witham Street. The farms there belonged to the Babson family, which included Ebenezer, a bachelor in his middle twenties, his mother, and several relatives. The events began at the end of June 1692 and started as odd sounds heard in the Babson house at night. But on July 7, things became more worrisome.

Ebenezer Babson arrived at his home late in the evening. As he approached the house, two men came out of the front door and ran into a nearby field. Startled, he hurried into the house to make sure that everything was all right, and his family told him that they had not seen the two men. If they had entered the house, they had done so without a sound.

Since he didn't recognize the strange men, Ebenezer took his rifle and followed them. He pushed his way through a field and approached a group of trees on the other side of it. As he got close, the two strangers suddenly emerged from behind a fallen log and ran into the nearby swamp. As they ran, Ebenezer heard one of them mutter, "The man of the house is come now, else we might have taken the house."

The men vanished into the darkness, and Ebenezer ran home, fearing that the two men had lured him away from the house so that others might attack his family. He was relieved to find that everything was peaceful at home, but he insisted that everyone pack their things and come with him to the fortified garrison in the village. On the way, he would warn others of the strange men.

Soon, the family, along with some of the other villagers, was locked into the garrison. They had just secured the door when they heard several men outside. Their voices were unfamiliar, and Ebenezer threw open the door to confront them with a pistol in hand. He spotted two men - perhaps the same two men - running down a hill and back into the swamp.

Confrontations of just this sort continued for the next month - defenders chasing the attackers, attackers chasing the defenders, with lots of shouting and firing of guns - but no one came close to actually capturing, or even getting a close look at, the mysterious men.

On the night of July 9, Ebenezer Babson was walking toward a meadow when two figures came running towards him. He later related that they looked like "Frenchmen." Since one of them was carrying a "bright gun" on his back, he retreated to the garrison. Locked inside, the settlers heard stamping and running outside and noises like stones being thrown against the walls.

Within days, the entire village was fortifying itself in the garrison each night. It was only here that they felt reasonably secure. The structure had thick walls of stone, two floors of solid wooden planks, narrow slits for rifles, and a fence of upright logs surrounding it. During the daylight hours, the villagers worked at their homes and fields with weapons close at hand and returned to the fortress at night.

For some time, no one but Ebenezer actually saw the attackers; they merely heard them. Then, toward the middle of July, Babson and a man named John Brown were in the garrison when three of the strange figures appeared. They fired at them with their muskets, but the men vanished into a cornfield. The men appeared and vanished repeatedly for hours, but the bullets fired by Babson and Brown never reached their intended targets. Both men were known for being better than average shots, but they were unable to hit the attackers.

On July 14, the villagers were in the garrison when a half-dozen of the strangers appeared at the edge of the fields. One of the men stayed behind in the garrison to watch over the families, and the others set off in pursuit of what they still assumed was a raiding party.

Two of the strangers ran out of the field, and Babson tried to fire at them, but his gun refused to go off. As the trigger clicked hollowly, he called out to his fellow Gloucester men, alerting them to the presence of the strangers. The other men came running to his position, and Babson saw three of the attackers emerge from the swamp. One of the men, he said, was wearing a white waistcoat. Ebenezer approached the three men within about 30 feet and attempted to fire his musket again. This time, it went off with a thunderous roar, and all three of the strangers fell to the ground. Somehow, he had managed to wound -- or kill -- all three of them with a single shot.

Or so he thought.

Babson ran toward the place where the men had fallen, and as he got close, all three men suddenly jumped to their feet, and one of the men fired a gun at him. The bullet buzzed past Babson's ear, and he ducked behind a tree to reload his musket. He called out to his friends, and the other villagers came running to his aid. As they approached, the strangers retreated toward a nearby field. Babson raised his gun and fired again, aiming for an attacker that was climbing over a wooden fence. The bullet struck him, and the man flipped over the fence to the other side, crashing into the corn. Babson and the other villagers ran to where the man had fallen - but he was gone. They searched the surrounding field and saw no trace of the man or his blood. He had simply vanished.

They searched for several minutes, and then an eerie sound began filtering through the corn. The sound of whispering chilled their blood. It seemed to come from all around them and was in a language that none recognized. Terrified, they retreated to the garrison and didn't venture out again that night, even when shadowy figures were seen lurking at the edge of the woods.

The trouble began again the next morning at sunrise. One of the attackers came out of the woods and stood at the edge of the field, within easy range of a musket shot. A man named Isaac Swan snatched up his long rifle and fired a shot, but it had no effect on the stranger. He simply turned and vanished back into the field.

The families in the garrison were paralyzed with fear. They needed help, and Ebenezer Babson volunteered to go down to the harbor. He planned to round up more men to launch an offensive against the raiders. As the others watched for the figures, Babson slipped out the door and began running toward the harbor. He had only traveled a short distance when he heard a gun go off. The bullet whistled past him, cut off a piece of a pine bush, and lodged into the trunk of a hemlock tree. Babson saw four men hurrying toward him, and he raised his musket and fired. Ducking off the trail, he plunged into the woods and kept running until he reached the seaport.

There, Ebenezer managed to convince six men to come back to the garrison with him, and they combed the woods as they walked back, looking for any sign of the strangers. They found the pine bush that had been clipped by the bullet and saw where it had lodged in the tree. One of the men dug it out with his knife and gave it to Babson. It seemed to be an ordinary musket ball, although it had been badly warped after impacting the tree trunk.

When they reached the garrison, Babson showed them the footprints that had been left by the strangers and related what had been happening at the edge of the village. As the men looked over the scene, one of them saw a man with long dark hair, pulled back and tied, and wearing a dark blue coat, standing at the edge of the woods. He pointed out the stranger, and the figure suddenly turned and disappeared into the woods. They chased after him, fired several shots without result, and briefly spotted another man who looked like a "Frenchman."

Several men, fitting the same description, were spotted later that same day by a man named John Hammond. He was scouting the edge of the woods and saw a figure wearing a blue shirt, white breeches, and "something about his head."

On July 17, several of the strangers approached the garrison, and although the men inside shot at them, the gunfire had no effect. Later that same day, Richard Dolliver and Benjamin Ellary left the garrison to try and spy on the strangers. What they saw was exceedingly odd. They claimed that several men came out of a nearby orchard, walking back and forth, and were using a stick to strike the house of John Rowe. Ellary noted that there were 11 men in the group. Dolliver raised his rifle and fired toward them, but none of them fell. The strangers simply turned and ran in the opposite direction.

The news of the strange happenings in Gloucester eventually reached Ipswich, and on July 18, 60 men were dispatched to try and assist with the situation. Among the men sent by Major Appleton was John Day, who later described his experiences. When the men arrived, they heard shots coming from the nearby woods, and they went in the direction of the sounds. John Day said that he saw a man with bushy black hair wearing a blue shirt running out of the woods in his direction. Day was close enough to shoot, but the woods were so thick that he couldn't get a clear aim. The bushy-haired man escaped, and Day went to a muddy spot to look for the man's footprints, but there was nothing there.

The presence of the small militia from Ipswich did nothing to disturb the attackers. They continued to appear almost every day. On July 25, Ebenezer Babson was in a field gathering his cattle and saw three of the figures standing on a point of rocks, looking out toward the sea. One of them had a gun strapped across his back. Babson decided to ambush the party. He crept silently through the bushes until he was less than 40 yards away from their position. He very carefully aimed his musket and pulled the trigger - but, once again, nothing happened. He pulled the trigger a dozen times, but the gun would not fire. At the sound of the trigger clicking, the three attackers turned and began slowly walking in Babson's direction. They did nothing to threaten him. In fact, aside from a few glances, they paid little attention to him. They passed by and vanished back into the forest.

This was the last time the strangers were seen. The villagers remained at the garrison for several more days, but the mysterious men did not return. Eventually, the militia decamped and returned to Ipswich, and the villagers of Gloucester slowly went back to their normal routine. The weird incidents of the mysterious men were soon only recalled as a strange oddity of the summer of 1692.

But who were these strange men? Where did they come from, and where did they go? Were they really French raiders, intent on menacing the people of Gloucester? If they were, a group of armed men spent nearly three weeks panicking the people of Gloucester for no apparent reason and at great risk to themselves. There was apparently nothing strange about the men's appearance. Their black hair and blue shirts were not uncommon, and neither was their speech, other than it was in an "unknown tongue." The settlers assumed they were French; however, no one ever reported hearing them speak in French. The only statement that anyone recognized was when Ebenezer Babson heard them say in plain English, "The man of the house is come...."

Assuming this was a hostile raiding party, why were no homes burned, no residents harmed, and no property stolen? Why were the raiders not reported anywhere else? Why was there no campsite ever found during the villagers' searches of the forest? The men surrounded the village for almost three weeks and left nothing behind but a few occasional footprints and a single bullet.

It was a very ineffectual raiding party if all they did was shoot at Ebenezer Babson a few times. The rest of their time they spent wandering around, banging on things, hitting John Rowe's house with a stick of some sort, and allowing the villagers to shoot at them and chase them into the woods.

But if they were not enemy soldiers, what were they? Were they supernatural figures of some sort? Some of the accounts that remain from 1692 seem to suggest this idea. The men appeared and disappeared, almost at will. They rarely left any sign behind. No bullets ever seemed to bother them, and, in most cases, guns aimed in their direction refused to fire. When Babson believed that he shot the man on the fence, he found no trace of a body or any sign of blood. Most Gloucester residents undoubtedly believed the men to be devilish creatures of some sort - they believed there was no other explanation for them.

And perhaps they were right. The mystery of these sinister strangers remains unsolved to this day.

THE "PHANTOM STABBER" OF BRIDGEPORT

Between February 1925 and May 1928, a menacing stranger held the city of Bridgeport, Connecticut, in a grip of terror. Throughout this period, a mysterious man was stabbing women on the streets, in parks, public buildings, even libraries, and churches. The wounds he inflicted were rarely serious. They seemed more designed to cause general panic than to do significant harm.

And if that was his goal - he certainly succeeded.

Even stranger, he was rarely seen, never identified, and never captured. His identity - and his motives - remains unknown today.

The stabbings began on February 20, 1925. Each incident was nearly the same - an unknown man, which none of the victims could offer a clear description of, approaches a woman and stabs her with a sharp knife, then hurries away. In several cases, the victims believed they had been slapped or punched until they saw the wound. None of the injuries were life-threatening or even particularly serious, but the attacks sent a ripple of fear throughout the community.

The Burroughs Memorial Library in Bridgeport, scene of the Stabber's first attack

The first victim was Mary Annunziato. The 12-year-old was waiting for a friend in the Burrough's Memorial Library lobby when a man brushed up against her. She had not seen or heard him approach, and he was gone before she could get a look at him. Just then, she felt a stinging sensation at her waist, put her hand down, and raised it to see it covered with blood. There was a neat cut - about four inches long - in her dress. A knife had cut through the cloth and slid along her stomach. Mary cried out and fell to the floor in a faint.

When she was taken to the hospital for treatment, doctors discovered that while the cut was not deep, it did require several stitches. The blade that had made it was razor-sharp.

It was a strange incident but seemed to be an isolated one - until April 22. Mildred Cook was in Bridgeport visiting relatives and was in the

Inside of the main branch of the post office, where Mildred Cook was stabbed by the Phantom

lobby of the U.S. Post Office when she felt a sharp pain in her breast. She reached up to the spot and found it wet. She then looked curiously at her hand, and the wetness was blood. There was a stab wound of about a quarter-inch deep and an inch wide in her breast.

The most baffling part of the attack was that she had seen no one near her at the time she felt the pain. The attacker had been so swift in his approach and exit that she had not noticed him.

The police didn't connect the two stabbings at the time, but when a third occurred precisely a month later, they realized they had a problem on their hands. Elsie Schwartz was standing in the lobby of the Burrough's Library and, like Mary Annunziato, was stabbed in the stomach by a mysterious assailant.

Detectives were put on the case, and officers were ordered to be on alert. Decoys were placed at the library and the post office, thinking the attacker might return to those spots, but nothing happened, and gradually the vigilance relaxed.

On August 22, the attacker returned. Edith Zimmerman, a 12-year-old from Philadelphia visiting relatives, was walking down James Street at 12:30 in the afternoon when a man

Downtown Bridgeport in the 1920s

bumped into her on the sidewalk. She didn't notice any pain - the knife being so sharp that it sliced right through her skin - but soon became aware of something warm running down her body. She ran the rest of the way to her relative's house, where it was discovered that she had been stabbed in the upper chest.

Things were now becoming tense in the city. The public was starting to realize that these were not isolated incidents. There was some sort of serial attacker on the loose in Bridgeport, and it didn't appear that he would stop until he was captured.

Less than a month after the last attack, Mary Dirgo, 16, was on her way back from lunch and stopped for a moment on the street in front of the Taylor Building in the commercial district. She saw what she described as a "dark young man" coming quickly toward her. As he went by, he bumped into her and forced her to take a step backward. She felt a sharp pain in her breast, but before she knew she had been stabbed, the man was gone.

On October 26, the attacker returned to the Burroughs Library and stabbed an 18-year-old girl named Dorothy Le Bari in the side.

Then, three days later, on October 29, the "Phantom Stabber," as the newspapers would start to call him, claimed his sixth victim. Margaret Nelson, 13, was stabbed in the right side of the back as she was walking home along Main Street. She felt something strike her and then saw a shadowy figure rush past and vanish down a side street. She went straight home and was later taken to the emergency hospital so her "slight wound" could be treated. The police were notified and searched the area around where the attack took place but found no clues.

On Friday, November 20, the Stabber struck again. A young woman named Jane Alexander was stabbed before she even knew what was happening.

On November 23, he struck again - two more times. His eighth and ninth victims were stabbed within minutes of each other and in the same neighborhood. Neither girl was seriously injured, and both were able to offer the first descriptions to the police, who were convinced the crimes had been the work of the same man who had committed the other attacks.

The first young woman stabbed that night was Catherine Dillon, who was 12-year-old. She was standing in front of her grandmother's house on Union Avenue, talking with a friend. Her grandfather and two of her uncles were in the backyard. According to her account, the Stabber ran across the street, quickly put an arm around the girl, and stabbed her in the right side. He immediately let go, pushing her into some bushes in front of the house, and ran off into the darkness.

At first, Catherine thought it was just a prank - played on her by a school friend - but then she realized that she was in pain. She clutched her side, and her hand came away, soaked with blood. She let out a scream and ran to the backyard, shouting to her grandfather and uncles that she had been stabbed.

They immediately spread the alarm. One of Catherine's uncles and her friend searched the neighborhood for over an hour but found no sign of him.

In the meantime, a doctor had been summoned and had bandaged Catherine's wound. It was less than an inch long and sliced into her right side, a short distance below her shoulder blade.

Just minutes after Catherine was stabbed, Rose Kerensky, also 12, was on her way home from the Newfield Branch Library with her little brother. They made it almost all the way to her home on Hollister Avenue when a man had appeared from the shadows and stabbed Rose in the side.

Rose's father, John, was also walking on the street at the same time as his children, coming from the opposite direction. He saw his daughter's assailant dart out from the side of the street and attack the girl. He rushed toward her with a loud cry, but the Stabber was too fast. He struck Rose with his knife and vanished.

At first, Rose didn't realize that she'd been stabbed. She thought she'd been accidentally stuck by a pin when the man bumped into her. It wasn't until she felt blood running down her side that she knew the man had stabbed her.

Rose was hurried home by her father, and a doctor was called. The physician who dressed the wound said it had occurred in almost the same place on the body where Catherine Dillon had been stabbed. He said it was "quite deep," but nothing to worry about.

These two attacks were the first time the Stabber had made a mistake - he'd allowed the victims to get a good look at him. Not only had Rose seen the man coming toward her on the sidewalk, but her brother had seen him dash away after the attack and jump onto a trolley heading for the station at the intersection of Hollister and Stratford Avenues. Both Rose and

"Phantom Stabber" Appears In City again, Strikes at Girl

Sudden Reappearance of Fiend, after Abstaining from Attacks Since December, Mystifies Police — Thirteen Year Old Girl Has Small Wound in Abdomen.

After several months inactivity Bridgeport's "phantom stabber" sprang into action last night about nine o'clock, and after slashing a

been pierced with a sharp instrument and in her abdomen was a small stab wound. Detectives were

her brother - as well as Catherine Dillon - offered the police a good description of the man.

They told detectives that he was about 40-year-old and appeared to be a "foreigner" -- which had a lot of different meanings in the 1920s but probably meant that he was dark-complected. He was also tall and slender and wore a brown hat that was creased in the center and a long brown overcoat.

All the witnesses assured the police that they would recognize him if they saw him again - but they never would.

The Phantom Stabber had disappeared again.

In the days that followed the two attacks, the police made a lot of noise about the "net" they were drawing tight on the mysterious attacker. The Department's detectives and patrolmen, the *Bridgeport Telegram* assured its readers, had received orders from Superintendent of Police Patrick Flanagan to concentrate all efforts "toward the apprehension of the fiend." While police officials would not comment on the steps they were taking to ensure the Stabber's capture, they wanted everyone to know that several "promising clues" had been uncovered.

If there really had been "promising clues" found, they didn't lead anywhere. The Stabber wasn't arrested - but he didn't attack anyone else for several weeks, striking once on December 12 and then again on December 22.

On that night, a young woman named Bertha Epilaski, age 17, had just left her home on Railroad Avenue and was walking to St. George's Lithuanian Church when a man rushed toward her from the street corner at South Avenue. He wrapped one arm around her, and Bertha said that he muttered a threat that he was going to stab her.

But the assailant had underestimated his potential victim. Bertha twisted in his grip, managed to get the man's arm away from her neck, and struck him at least twice. As she did so, she screamed for help, catching the attention of several nearby pedestrians. Unnerved by the fight and the girl's calls for help, the Stabber let go of Bertha and ran off into the night.

The people on the street who had heard her call out hurried to her side, but the Stabber was gone by the time they arrived. No one had gotten a good look at him, but Bertha believed he had been wearing a sheepskin coat.

Somehow, Bertha had made it through the struggle without a scratch - but others would not be so lucky.

The Stabber dropped out of sight for almost eight months after the attempted attack on Bertha Epilaski. The police and the newspapers often revisited the past stabbings and pledged to solve the crimes, but interest began to fade as winter turned to spring and then became summer.

Then on August 5, 1926, he was back. That evening around 9:00 p.m., Mary Corcoran, 13, was walking home along Lyon Terrace with her younger brother when she noticed a man walking toward them. He tipped his hat to two women who passed him, but when he met up with Mary on the sidewalk, he suddenly grabbed her and struck her in the stomach.

The man then pushed her away and ran across the street, where he turned around to watch Mary and her brother. Mary was in pain and confused but didn't want to anger the man by confronting him. Instead, they hurried home.

Mary had no idea that she had been stabbed.

When she arrived home, she told her mother that a stranger had punched her in the stomach. This sent a chill through Mrs. Corcoran. She had followed the exploits of the "Phantom Stabber" in the community last year and insisted on examining her daughter's stomach. She quickly found that Mary's clothing had been cut by some sharp object - and there was a stab wound in her abdomen.

The Corcorans immediately called the police, and Mary was rushed to the Emergency Hospital, where the wound was cauterized and pronounced "not serious."

When Mary spoke with the police, she described the Stabber as five-foot-eight-inches, with pale skin and a light-colored suit. This didn't seem to match the descriptions from victims in late 1925. Was it the same man? Or some sort of copycat attacker?

No one knew, but the police weren't taking any chances. The return of the Stabber after months of inactivity shocked the city. They demanded action, and the police complied - dozens of suspects were questioned, but no one was arrested. The attacker had, as always, left no clues behind.

Panic gripped Bridgeport now that the Stabber was back. People began to imagine seeing him on every corner - even though no one really knew what he looked like - and the police switchboard was deluged with calls. Detectives and officers were soon exhausted from chasing down leads that led nowhere.

But they would have to wait long for the Stabber to strike again.

On Friday, August 13, the Stabber attacked two more girls, raising the victim toll once again. It had been a dark night, and the attacker had used the cover of falling rain to claim his two victims within minutes of each other.

The two young women were Anna Borggard, 26, who was stabbed on Broad Street, and Mary Lenitto, 14, who was attacked a short distance away on State Street. They were both treated by Dr. C.E. Haberlin, who theorized that the knife the attacker used was a stiletto due to the deep but narrow wounds left behind.

Anna was the first to encounter the Stabber. She had been at her hairdresser's shop on Broad Street and was just starting toward home when she was stabbed.

It was raining, and she had her umbrella open, so she paid little attention to the man walking toward her until he passed, and she felt a sharp pain in her side. She quickly realized that she had been stabbed, but by then, the man had vanished around the corner.

Anna cried out for help, catching the attention of E.O. Williksen, a motorist who was parked on the street. He quickly got out of his car and hurried to her aid. As Anna tried breathlessly to tell him what had occurred, he was getting her into his car and taking her to police headquarters. From there, an ambulance took her to the hospital, where Dr. Haberlin treated her. Although questioned by detectives, she could not give a clear description of the man who attacked her.

When Williksen and Anna Borggard arrived at the police station, they arrived at the same time as the other victim, Mary Lenitto.

Earlier in the evening, Mary had been with her friend, Stella Hodoska, at the home of Stella's aunt, Mrs. Shugura, on Prospect Street. Heavy rain started while the two girls were there, so Mrs. Shugura suggested they stay the night. But when the rain slackened around 9:00 p.m., they decided to walk home. They had just turned onto State Street when a man came running toward them.

The two girls were walking side by side on the sidewalk, with Mary on the man's left as he sprinted in their direction. They moved aside so he could pass between them, and as he did, he swiftly stabbed Mary in the left breast. The force of the blow knocked the young woman back on her heels, and she yelled after the man - just as Stella noticed the bloodstain spreading on her dress. She began screaming for help.

Inside the building, a young steeplejack - a craftsman who scales buildings, chimneys, and church steeples to carry out repairs or maintenance - named Ernest Noel was listening to his Victrola next to his open window. He heard the screams coming from the sidewalk below at a pause between songs on a record. He looked out the window, saw the two girls, and without a thought, jumped out the window of his second-floor apartment to help them.

Ernest was an agile man, who was used to working on steep roofs and buildings, but he didn't fare so well at his own apartment. His foot got tangled in a vine that was growing up the side of the brick wall, and he pitched forward, landing 14 feet below on his hands and knees. To make matters worse, he stumbled as he got up, and his foot went through a basement window and cut his leg. When he made sure that the two girls were all right, he started after their attacker. The Stabber had a head start on him, but Ernest gamely gave chase anyway.

As Ernest turned a corner in pursuit, he saw the man duck into a driveway on Warren Street. Ernest started searching the backyards of the neighborhood but found no sign of him. Officer Julius Dorkin joined him in the search after the police had been called, and together, they looked in outbuildings and vacant houses for any trace of the Stabber - but he had vanished.

By the time the search was called off, Ernest had bled through his socks and pants. The cut he'd received when his foot went through the basement window was deep, but he refused treatment while the search for the attacker was going on. Eventually, detectives arrived from headquarters, and Ernest was sent to the hospital.

The Phantom Stabber had eluded everyone again - and he still wasn't finished that night.

Although there is little information about this attack, the phantom also stabbed a 16-year-old girl named Adeline Kinder on the night of August 13. Her name was added to the tally of victims, which sent the city into an uproar once again.

Superintendent Flanagan canceled all days off for his officers until the Stabber was captured. He announced that every effort would be made to bring the man to justice, and the department wouldn't rest until he was behind bars. Detectives working in plainclothes made several arrests over the following weekend, including of a man who was arrested in a theater for "annoying a woman." Another man questioned was the mentally unstable brother of a librarian, who worked where one of the early attacks occurred. Both men were soon released.

The Stabber had vanished again.

On October 7, he was back, and this time, he claimed a victim at a church. Carmella Charalla, 19, was on her way into St. Augustine's Church with her friend, Emma Tuccello, for evening mass. When the two girls entered through the south entrance, a man was coming down the stairs toward them. Emma had walked through the door first, but Carmella stopped to hold the door open for the man. She said that he was blessing himself when she looked up at him, and his hand was on his forehead, making the sign of the cross, so she didn't get a good look at his face.

As she stepped aside to let him pass, the man suddenly lurched against her and then hurried down the outside steps and disappeared into the darkness. Carmella felt a stinging pain in her left side and saw that blood was seeping through her dress - she had been stabbed.

Emma hurried over to her, and without making an outcry, the girls left the church and went to the nearby office of Dr. Rowe. When he saw what had occurred, he quickly telephoned the police. By the time they arrived, though, the man was long gone.

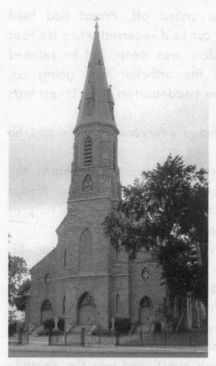

St. Augustine's Church, where Carmella Charalla was stabbed by the Phantom

Both young women - as well as a male parishioner who witnessed the attack, although didn't realize what had happened at the time - gave a description of the man to detectives. They said he was about 30-years-old, slender, at least six feet tall, with a smooth face. He was wearing a gray suit and hat.

This seems to have been at least the third varying description of the Stabber - was there more than one of them at work in Bridgeport? It seems unlikely, based on his *modus operandi*, but I suppose anything is possible.

The attacks continued, and so did the panic. False alarms were raised - some maliciously, others by mistake - and sightings of the Stabber kept the police busy in the latter months of 1926. Suspects were questioned and released. Arrests were made, and men were set free when there was no evidence to hold them.

Read's Department store in downtown Bridgeport, where two of the Stabber's attacks took place.

The Phantom Stabber was everywhere - and nowhere.

On October 23, Margaret Bruzinski was hurrying out of Read's Department Store on her way to a picture show. She had just gotten off work at the store and had gone to the employee locker room to get her hat and coat. On a stair landing, she ran into a man who grabbed her around the neck, put a hand over her mouth, and stabbed her in the left breast.

The Stabber then released her and vanished out of the store, passing by numerous customers and employees as he went. No one got a good look at him.

Weeks passed in silence. There were no more attacks. The Phantom Stabber had gone on hiatus once again. But to the dismay of Superintendent Flanagan, he didn't stay away for good.

He returned on February 5 and claimed his twenty-first victim, Charlotte Mosseau. The girl had gone out to mail a letter, and on her way home, a man rushed out at her from a side alley, wrapped his arms around her, and slashed her cheek two times. Charlotte fainted and was found unconscious on the sidewalk a few moments later.

A special edition of the New York American detailed the crimes of the Phantom Stabber when the victim toll reached 16. The editors had no idea at the time just how many victims the unknown assailant would eventually claim.

"No trace of the Stabber was found," read the police report on the incident. It had been that way now for two years, and the police were no closer to catching the man than they had been in 1925.

This time, the Stabber was quiet until July 26, when he claimed his next victim in broad daylight. Selma Ginsburg, 16, was on her way to summer classes at Central High School when a man on the street attacked her. Bleeding from her left breast, she staggered into the school and called for help. She was rushed to the hospital for treatment and afterward taken home.

She told the police that she had casually noticed a man follow her across the street but had thought nothing of it until, in passing her, he quickly lunged at her, and she felt a sharp pain. In a moment, the man was gone.

A month later, on August 27, the Stabber claimed another victim. Isabelle Pelskur, 14, was a messenger girl at Read's Department Store downtown, where Margaret Bruzinski had been stabbed. Isabelle was ascending a staircase when a man came up behind her and slashed her across the back.

The attack occurred as the crowd of shoppers was leaving the store at closing time. Whoever the attacker was, he blended into the mass of people unobserved and made his escape.

The phantom was back again on September 29. This time, he attacked Ruth Stillings, 14, a pretty high school tennis star. She was stabbed in the right breast on her way home from Blardsley Park. Within minutes, the police had surrounded the park, but the assailant was long gone.

Ruth became the 24th victim of the Phantom Stabber.

On December 7, 1927, he struck again. Estelle Haupler, an 18-year-old married mother of a seven-month-old baby, was attacked on Pequannock Street and stabbed in the right breast. Bleeding badly, she ran to the Leverty Drug Store, and the pharmacist there called the police.

A squad of police officers, led by Assistant Superintendent Thomas Flood and Captain John Regan of the Detective Bureau, were on the scene in minutes, but there was no trace of the Stabber.

According to Estelle's account, she was walking along the street around 5:30 p.m. when a short, heavily built man in a brown overcoat and cap brushed past her. She felt a stinging pain and realized he had stabbed her with a long, thin blade. She screamed as the man hurried across the street and disappeared between two buildings.

The police went into action once again. Superintendent Flanagan canceled all leaves and days off, ordering the men to comb the city in a manhunt for the phantom. Telephone calls from panicked Bridgeport residents clogged the lines with tips and reports of "suspicious" and "foreign-looking" men in every neighborhood in the city. Flanagan and the department were under increased scrutiny after more than two years of inability to capture the Stabber. Reverend Edward Mason McKinley, the well-known rector of the Trinity Methodist Church, had publicly denounced the department for their failure to find the phantom. Interviews with the minister in the newspaper had presented the police poorly, adding more stress and urgency to the investigation - an investigation that was still going nowhere.

Then, on December 13, the Phantom Stabber indirectly added another victim to his ever-growing list - Police Superintendent Patrick Flanagan. The chief died from a heart attack during the early morning hours, and his doctor insisted it had been caused by overwork as he tried to track down the attacker. Flanagan had simply refused to retire until the case had been solved. He told friends that he'd capture the Stabber, even if it killed him. The investigation did kill him, but the phantom was no closer to being caught.

And then suddenly, he was. Well, a Stabber was caught. It just wasn't *the* Stabber that all of Bridgeport was looking for.

His name was Lorenzo Desmarais, and he was 17-years-old. He was a transient, living in a boarding house on Front Street in Hartford, Connecticut, which had recently been the scene of three stabbing attacks, possibly by the same man who had been attacking women in Bridgeport for the previous two years. He was arrested by the police and picked out of a line-up by the three women he had attacked.

It should come as no surprise that detectives from Bridgeport hurried to Hartford to be present when Desmarais was questioned. Lorenzo quickly confessed to the attacks in Hartford, then added that he had lived in Bridgeport for a time, hinting that he might have information that the police

The dim-witted Lorenzo Desmarais stabbed a few women in Hartford and then confessed to being the Phantom Stabber of Bridgeport, even though he was only 14 when the attacks began. He would eventually be committed to a mental hospital.

wanted. But all of that turned out to be a lie. Lorenzo was living with his family in Massachusetts before moving to Hartford with his parents. He had only been 14 at the time of the first Bridgeport attack in 1925, which quickly ruled him out.

His only connection to the Bridgeport attacks? He wanted to stab more women in Hartford than the record held by Bridgeport's "Phantom Stabber."

Lorenzo's time in court was short. He was quickly diagnosed as insane by a commission of doctors and was committed to the Connecticut State Hospital at Middletown.

Perhaps just to grab back the headlines from Lorenzo Desmarais, the *real* Stabber stuck again in Bridgeport on April 21, 1928.

The attack took place at 2:15 in the afternoon in front of Lakeview Cemetery on Boston Avenue. The victim was Janet Clark, 13, a freshman at Warren Harding High School. She was walking down the street and was reaching up to fix a button on the left shoulder of her coat when she was stabbed. Apparently aiming for her breast, the knife struck her in the hand.

The attack was never reported to the police, but it did earn a single mention in the newspaper at the time. If the press had known there would only be one more attack in the Stabber's career, they might have paid more attention.

The Phantom Stabber's final victim was attacked on May 31, 1928. Anna Rauch, 24, was an employee of the Bridgeport Coach Lace Company and was on her way to work around 7:00 a.m. when she encountered the phantom on Colorado Avenue.

The attacker was hiding in some bushes along the sidewalk, and when Anna passed by, he lurched forward and tried to stab her in the left breast. Luckily for Anna, she had her purse under her left arm, bending her arm so that her sleeve covered her breast. The knife cut through the cloth and lining of her coat and lacerated the skin of her forearm. She stumbled from the force of the blow, and the man ran away.

Anna was close to the home of a friend, Mrs. Henry Bergen, and went there to have the wound treated. Her friend called Dr. Alfred Kornblut to care for the cut, and he called the police. Within minutes, several officers were at the scene, and they started a search for the Stabber.

It was called off after no clues were found.

"No clues were found" - words that became a theme for the three-year rampage of Bridgeport's Phantom Stabber. Who was he? And why was he so difficult to catch? By the 1920s, police investigation techniques had improved dramatically. Fingerprinting and photography were standard tools in almost every department in the country, as were early forensic methods, so why were no clues ever found?

The Bridgeport phantom is an anomaly in the annals of unsolved mysteries. Unlike so many attackers, he was violent, but he never killed anyone. His victims were always women, and even though they were traumatized, none of them were badly wounded. It appears the Stabber was more interested in causing panic and fear than really hurting anyone. If I had to guess, I'd say that this was his way of dominating his female victims. You don't have to be a psychiatrist to get the idea that his knife, when carefully penetrating these women, was a stand-in for sex.

It's also notable that most - although not all - of his attacks occurred within about a month between them. Occasionally, even a longer stretch between attacks occurred, but he always returned. Perhaps he could only resist his urges for so long. We'll never know.

The Phantom Stabber was almost undoubtedly a man with some deviant urges, but some suggest he may not have been one man. There were several different descriptions of the attacker given by different witnesses. Could there have been several attackers? And if so, were they working separately or together? Even if there was more than one man, the attacks had to be coordinated in some way. Based on the signature of the attacks, it was one man - or it was a group who was carefully planning them.

This is definitely one of the strangest stories I have ever worked on, but when discussing it with a few others, they have suggested that there may be more to this story than first meets the eye. Who was the Stabber? How did he manage to get away so easily? How did he disappear and leave no clues behind? He showed up in Bridgeport, wreaked havoc on and off for three years, and then vanished as if he'd never been there at all. Did he step back into his own time and place one day and leave ours forever.

I don't know.

But I have to say that stories like this make me wonder just how many things are going on in our world that we will never truly understand.

THE BUNNY UNDER THE BRIDGE

Urban legends are interesting things.

No matter what they involve, whether it's murdered babysitters, hook-handed killers, or sinister figures who hang out under bridges, almost all of them have some element of truth to them. As I like to say: these stories got started for a reason.

Take, for instance, the legend of "Charlie No-Face" in Western Pennsylvania. If you grew up in the Pittsburgh area in the 1950s and 1960s, you knew the story.

There was a man, the story went, who stalked the desolate highways at night, waiting to terrify anyone foolish enough to seek him out. The man had been nearly burned alive in an accident; his face melted like candle wax. Or maybe he had been struck by lightning when he was a boy. Or maybe his flesh melted, and his skin turned radioactive green after a horrible accident at the Duquesne Power Plant.

The details often changed, depending on who was telling the story of the sinister stranger known as "Charlie No-Face" or the "Green Man" or, worst of all, the "Monster of Beaver County." Most assumed it was merely a legend, no matter how many claimed they had met the mysterious figure growing up or saw him along a roadway at night.

But Charlie No-Face was not a myth. He was a real person - and his name was actually Ray.

In August 1919, Ray Robinson was eight-years-old and was accidentally electrocuted by a stray power cable. Thousands of volts went through his body. He was severely electrocuted and fell to the ground. His nose, lips, and ears were misshapen by the shock - or were gone altogether. His arms were twisted and maimed, and one of his hands was blown completely off. The pain he suffered was unimaginable.

The shock should have killed him, but it didn't. Somehow, he survived, but his life was never the same. Ray was never mistreated, but he was isolated and ostracized, even by his own family, who refused to eat meals with him.

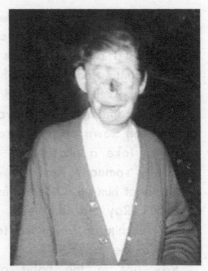

Ray Robinson, the man who became known as "Charlie No-Face"

Ray made the best of it. He was an avid baseball fan and listened to every game he could find on the radio dial. When he grew up, his family built a small apartment for him in the garage to have a little independence.

It was a sad, lonely existence. For the most part, Ray stayed out of sight, never asking or seeking any kind of attention. Most likely, few would have ever known that he existed if not for a habit that he picked up of walking the local highways at night when no one could see his face.

And that was when Ray became a legend.

Ray started walking the roads at night, most along Route 351 but other places in Beaver County, too. And people started to notice. Word spread about the "faceless" man who wandered along the quiet roads, and people began to seek him out to see if the story was true.

It was. And the moniker "Charlie No-Face" was born.

Ray didn't mind the strangers who searched him out at night for the most part. He liked to smoke and drink beer - two things often offered by the "Charlie No-Face" tourists and the late-night encounters on the side of the road became one of his main connections to the wider world.

The encounters didn't always go well. Not everyone who tracked him down on a backroad was content to share a beer with him, take a photo, and move on. As everyone knows - especially someone like Ray - the world can be cruel. Some people beat him up. Others urinated into beer bottles, then gave it to him. Ray learned never to accept an open drink. Some would pick him up, drive him to an isolated spot, and then kick him out of the car.

Ray got in the habit of being anxious when a car approached him during his nighttime walks. He stopped and waited nervously to see what happened next. Eventually, the story goes, Ray started carrying a pistol in his belt, thanks to one nasty encounter.

But for the most part, Ray's interactions with people were kind and generous. Everyone who actually met him always spoke of him as a warm, friendly man. Photographs of Ray that remain show a man who was happy and companions who weren't scared of how he looked. He taught a lot of people about what it was like to be different and the need to look past surface appearances for what was underneath.

Ray was never angry about how his life turned out. He was a positive person with many people who cared about him - people he would never have met without his nightly sojourns along the dark highways of Western Pennsylvania.

So, how did this kind, well-liked man go on to become a terrifying legend?

For more than 40 years, teenagers who live in Western Pennsylvania have taken to the roads at night in search of a monster - "Charlie No-Face." Few can tell you of his history, only that he's out there, waiting in the darkness to be found.

Some say he is a ghost.

Others say he is a man.

He appears in the darkness, along the side of the road, stalking thrill-seekers who are brave enough to try and find him.

The legends say that if you enter a tunnel -- or park on a bridge, or pull over on a certain road, the stories vary - turn off your car, take out your keys, and place them on the road for a few minutes, you'll find the car won't start when it's time to leave. But if you call out the name of "Charlie No-Face" three times or flash your headlights three times, the mysterious figure will appear and chase you away.

Of course, it's ridiculous, and no one really thinks this story is true. They simply seek out the ghost, or monster, or whatever "Charlie No-Face" is for a bit of thrill and a good, scary time on a Saturday night in a place that's not exactly known for its nightlife.

Are the stories of this sinister stranger doing a disservice to the memory of a man who lived a simple life and just wanted to have friends? Perhaps, but then again, maybe the real "Charlie" wouldn't mind.

As I said, urban legends are interesting. The truth behind them is often tragic. Ray Robinson's face was unforgettable. He had a reputation as a man who scared people, and he still does even today.

Ray was a real person who became a legend.

Can the same be said for a man in a bunny suit?

For decades now, people have been flocking to a spot off the highway in Fairfax County, Virginia, in search of a sinister stranger. They come to a railroad overpass that has the unofficial name of the "Bunny Man Bridge."

The railroad overpass in Fairfax County, Virginia that has become known as "Bunny Man Bridge."

There is a story behind the bridge, although its elements often change. The bridge is the lair of a man in a bunny costume with an ax who attacks motorists near the underpass. Although sometimes his victims aren't motorists, and sometimes the Bunny Man doesn't have an ax. And sometimes, he's a ghost. And sometimes, he's not even wearing a bunny costume.

Some versions of the legend say that the Bunny Man was once a local hermit who lived near the bridge in the 1940s. The former mental patient was popular with children in the area, especially since he dressed in a bunny costume every Halloween. One day, though, he snapped and murdered one of the kids. He later died in prison, and his ghost - wearing the bunny suit he loved so much - has been haunting the place ever since.

Another variation of the tale claims that a local resident dressed up in a bunny costume one Halloween night and murdered his wife and children, but then opened the door to trick-or-treaters for the rest of the night while the bodies of his family were still in the house. He's still out there, the stories say, lurking near the bridge, waiting to claim more victims.

And there's more - another version claims that the Bunny Man was a patient at an insane asylum in Lorton, Virginia, back in the 1930s. When it closed, the inmates were shuttled by bus to a new hospital farther south. The story says that the bus crashed during the trip, and several patients escaped. All but two of them were found a short time later. The police searched for the missing patients for months but only found rabbit carcasses near an old railroad bridge in the woods. Then one day, one of the inmates was discovered, hanging from the bridge, gutted, with a knife near his feet. The other patient was never found. Since that time, it's said, there have been at least ten documented murders at the site, all between the 1950s and 1980s. They were committed by the last patient - the man dubbed the "Bunny Man."

I know what you're thinking - impossible to believe, right? And no, there are no "documented murders" attributed to an escaped mental patient either. I promised there was some truth behind the story of this mysterious figure, but nothing you've read so far qualifies.

So, what is it? Who really was the Bunny Man, and why did he lurk around this lonely stretch of roadway? The origins of this unsettling story seem to date back to October 1970, when several incidents occurred to create the legend of the Bunny Man.

The first incident involved an Air Force Academy cadet named Robert Bennett and his fiancée. The couple were parked on Guinea Road in the town of Burke, Virginia. They had driven there after a football game to visit Robert's uncle, who lived across the street. While they were sitting in the car with the engine running, the right front window was suddenly smashed with a hatchet.

A man wearing "something white over his head" had run out of the bushes behind the car and struck the window with the hatchet. He shouted at them, "You're on private property, and I have your tag number!"

Of course, Robert slammed the car in gear, stomped on the gas, and sped away, taking the hatchet with him since it was now inside the car.

While the story claimed that Robert reported the man was wearing a "white suit with bunny ears," his fiancée reported that it looked like the man was wearing a peaked white hood.

The second incident occurred ten days later. A security guard named Paul Phillips was patrolling an under-construction housing development called King's Park West, which was also along Guinea Road when he came upon a man wearing a bunny suit. The costumed man was standing on the porch of an unfinished home, chopping at one of the porch posts with an ax.

There was no question about the description this time. Phillips definitively described the man as wearing a "white bunny suit with floppy ears." When Phillips approached the man, he turned to threaten the guard. "You are trespassing," he said. "If you come any closer, I'll chop off your head."

Before Phillips could react, the man turned and ran off into the nearby woods, leaving a lot of questions in his wake.

These two incidents on their own would have been quickly forgotten but with the two together - with shared details like a hatchet, accusations of trespassing, and a possible bunny costume - people started talking.

A reporter from the *Washington Star* newspaper interviewed several area residents to get their reaction to the report about the man in the bunny suit. He quickly found they were amused - and a little afraid.

After reports of the incidents appeared in the newspapers, people began coming out to the subdivision to get a look at the chopped post. Cars drove up and down the streets at all hours, hoping to get a glimpse of the Bunny Man.

It wasn't long before the Fairfax County Police had to open an investigation into the incident because they had been flooded with more than 50 calls from people who claimed to see a man in a white bunny suit. The stories spread - and got wilder all the time. In one newspaper interview, a resident claimed that the Bunny Man had eaten their missing cat.

Things cooled off soon after that, but the following autumn marked the return of the Bunny Man. It was reported that three Maryland children on their way home from school had seen "this man on the street with this bunny suit on with a hatchet." Police responded to a call from one of the children's mothers, but they found nothing when they searched the areas. There were three such calls that followed over the next couple of weeks, all in the Washington, D.C. suburbs.

It should be noted, though, that a check of area costume rental agencies discovered that several large-size bunny outfits had been rented by men around the time of these incidents. Coincidence? Probably not.

More sightings followed, however, and they still do today, which has kept the story of the Bunny Man alive. He has allegedly been spotted in Virginia, all over the Washington, D.C. area, and in at least a dozen communities in Maryland.

And then, of course, there is the railroad overpass in Clifton, Virginia - the site where one of the escaped mental patients supposedly killed the other one and left him hanging from the bridge. After committing the "documented murders" of the story, police launched a manhunt for the missing inmate. He was eventually cornered on the railroad tracks above - you guessed it - the eerie overpass. He was struck and killed by a train while trying to make his getaway, and his spirit, so the story goes, has haunted the place ever since.

So, here's a tale of a sinister stranger that might be worth taking with a grain of salt. But just remember, as I keep trying to tell you, no matter how crazy some of the stories are that you might hear - they all got started for a reason.

In other words, you may want to stay away from grown men in bunny suits, just in case.

THE PHANTOM BARBER OF PASCAGOULA

One of the strangest series of crimes in American history - which is saying a lot - occurred in the town of Pascagoula, Mississippi, in the 1940s and involved a sinister stranger, unlike anything we have seen before.

This particular figure had a penchant for home invasion and prowling around in young girls' bedrooms. Luckily, he wasn't a killer. No throats were cut, and no one was murdered in their bed.

This mysterious stranger had a creepy habit of cutting locks of hair off the girls while they slept.

The Japanese attack on Pearl Harbor in December 1941 plunged America into World War II. It was a time of uncertainty, terror, and a shaken faith in the fact that the United States was invincible to its enemies. As young men went off to fight the war overseas, women were left behind to take over the responsibilities and jobs that men had once held. Small towns all over the country were transformed into producers of everything needed for the war effort.

Pascagoula was one of those towns. The construction of warships turned the little fishing community into a boomtown in the early days of the war. The population of roughly 5,000 souls tripled, seemingly overnight. The larger population meant a boost to the local economy, but it also meant that the police

Building ships in Pascagoula during World War II. Everyone knew the Germans and the Japanese were the enemy, but no one expected to have to deal with something sinister at home

department began struggling to keep the newcomers in line. And in addition to the expected rise in break-ins, petty crime, and drunken brawls, the Pascagoula police were forced to deal with another menace - the so-called "Phantom Barber."

The first "attack" occurred on June 5, 1942. Mary Evelyn Briggs and Edna Marie Hydel shared a room at the Our Lady of Victories convent and were shocked when they awoke to see a man in their room. Mary Evelyn turned out to be the only witness who ever got a look at the Barber. She told a reporter, "I saw the figure of a kinda short fat man bending over me with something shiny in his hand, and he was fooling with my hair. When he saw me open my eyes, he said 'shhh'... I yelled... and he jumped out the window."

The girls both turned out to be unharmed - although frightened - and each was missing a lock of their hair.

The intrusion into the bedroom of two young girls set the community on edge - or perhaps *more* on edge would be more accurate. Everyone in the country was already pretty paranoid, and towns like Pascagoula, which were becoming vital to the war effort, had to wonder if they were an enemy target. With all the new people and faces in town, some questioned how many of them might be spies. A weird attack like this one made people feel unsafe, even in their own homes.

Over the weekend that followed the nonconsensual hair clippings, news and gossip spread with people adding and embellishing the details. Things became so bad that a later newspaper report even mentioned ten attacks by the Barber - a number he never reached.

But the attacks that did happen were bad enough.

The Barber struck again on Monday, June 8. Late that night, he cut a slit in the window screen of the Peattie family home, managed to get into the house, and snipped off a lock of six-year-old Carol Peattie's hair as she was asleep next to her twin brother. The barber left behind a single clue when he fled the scene - a footprint in the sand outside the window.

The following incident occurred a few nights later, on June 12. Terrell Heidelberg and his wife were asleep when the Barber - or someone else -- sliced open the window screen and entered the house. This time, he didn't cut anyone's hair. Instead, he attacked the couple with an iron pipe, striking Mrs. Heidelberg hard enough in the mouth that she lost several teeth. Terrell Heidelberg was knocked unconscious by the blows. It all happened so quickly that neither of them got a good look at their attacker.

The police investigated the break-in as thoroughly as they could, even bringing in dogs to try and follow the attacker's trail. The dogs managed to find a pair of bloodstained gloves in the woods, but nothing else. The theory was that the Barber might have stashed a bicycle in the woods that he used for his escape.

The Heidelbergs recovered from the attack, but concern in the community had turned to panic. Men and women began refusing to work the night shift because they needed to stay home and protect their family - or at least their family's hair. This had a direct impact on the war effort, but the police were at a loss as to what to do. They eventually decided to offer a $300 reward for information, but it generated no new leads.

The final attack occurred on Sunday night, June 14, at the home of the Taylor family. Mrs. R.E. Taylor, who was asleep in a bedroom with her husband and two daughters, reported that an intruder had cut off two inches of her hair.

She had been awakened by a smell. "I had a vague feeling of something passing over my face," she said. The next thing she knew, she woke up feeling violently ill. The police later determined that the Barber had cut through the window screen, stuck a rag soaked with chloroform over Mrs. Taylor's face, and then cut off the lock of her hair.

Pressure was mounting on law enforcement to find the attacker, but they simply had no leads. Another month passed with residents living in fear before the authorities suddenly announced they had caught the Phantom Barber.

His name, the police said, was William Dolan. He was a 57-year-old chemist who had fought with Terrell Heidelberg's father, a local magistrate, over a legal issue. It was thought that he had attacked the couple for revenge. And maybe he did - but how did this tie him to the attacks during which the intruder clipped young girls' hair?

That was easily solved. The police claimed that when they searched his house, a large bundle of human hair was found behind his home. Oh, and some of it looked like it matched the Carol Peattie, the Barber's youngest victim. The FBI later confirmed it - little Carol's hair was mixed in with what was found.

Dolan insisted that he was innocent but was quickly found guilty of attempted murder and sentenced to spend the next ten years in prison. He was never charged with any crimes connected to the hair clipping incident, but as far as the public was concerned, the Phantom Barber had been captured, and it was safe now to go back to work and keep building ships for the war effort.

Nothing to worry about here, right?

In 1948, Mississippi's Governor Fielding Wright reviewed the case against William Dolan and found a few issues with it. He asked Dolan to agree to a lie detector test, which he did and passed with flying colors. Governor Wright granted Dolan a suspended sentence, and he was set free in 1951.

What had the governor seen when he looked at the file? It was probably what many others have seen when looking back at the case - that Dolan was not the Phantom Barber.

His arrest came at a time when the public was in a state of panic, and the police were desperate to close the case. It would have been very easy -- after picking up Dolan for the Heidelberg attack, during which no one's hair had been cut - to plant the hair at his house and then tamper with the evidence that was sent to the FBI for analysis. Also, remember that the hair was found *outside* the house - anyone could have put it there. It didn't have to be planted by the police. It could have been left there by the actual Barber.

Since Dolan probably did commit the break-in at the Heidelberg home, and it occurred when other break-ins were going on, it was easy to connect this incident to the others.

There's no question that the governor realized that Dolan's case had been rushed because it had been linked to the Phantom Barber incidents. Even though he was not charged with the attacks, they had undoubtedly been in the mind of the jury, which likely encouraged them to find him guilty.

And a connection to the Barber attacks may not have been the only thing that influenced the verdict against William Dolan.

Dolan was German, had attended university in Germany before the war, and was a known German sympathizer. Many people in town considered him a traitor. There is no question that this also influenced the case against him.

It's nearly certain that William Dolan was not the Phantom Barber. But if he wasn't, then who was? And why did the attacks stop? Did the real Barber decide to stop after Dolan was prosecuted? Or did he simply move on to another town where his crimes went unnoticed?

It's impossible to say, but for a short time in 1942, the Phantom Barber of Pascagoula was an enigma that not only baffled the police and frightened the people of the city - he also directly affected the American war effort, too.

THE BLUE MAN OF LOUISVILLE

In January 1921, a very unusual sort of visitor arrived in the city of Louisville, Kentucky. He hung around for about a month, overstaying his welcome and making a nuisance of himself before suddenly departing just as mysteriously as he arrived.

Today, most people have forgotten about the brief tenancy of the "Blue Man" in Louisville, but during the time it was taking place, it was just about all anyone could talk about.

The "Blue Man" apparently arrived at some point in early January. He'd already made an impression on people, especially those who lived and worked around Eighth and Kentucky Streets downtown, by the time the *Courier-Journal* newspaper began a series of stories about him on January 17.

Downtown Louisville in the 1920s

In that first story, a reporter from the paper interviewed Reese Carrell, who had encountered a figure that he said was extremely tall and had a face that appeared to be blue - hence the moniker that would soon be pinned on the stranger.

"I've only been knocked down once in my life, and it did it," Reese stated. "It's been around here every night for the last two weeks. What it's after, I don't know. But one-night last week when I came home at about 11 o'clock, I saw somebody standing on our front step. I thought it was my father, and I walked right up to him. 'Looking for the Blue Man, Pop?' I asked him, and just then, he hit me in the chest. I was knocked against the fence, and when I got up, it was gone."

Around the same time as the attack on Reese Carrell, Mrs. Earl Schubnell also encountered the "Blue Man." Around 8:30 p.m. on the previous Thursday night, she was sitting in her kitchen and heard the shutter of one of the windows moving, after which a hand reached through a broken pane in the window.

"The hand caught hold of the curtain and pulled it back," Mrs. Schubnell told a reporter. "But when I screamed, it was withdrawn quickly, and I heard the sound of someone running out of the alley and down the street in the direction of Kentucky Street." In contrast to Carrell's description, Mrs. Schubnell said

'Blue Man' Seen At Eighth and Walnut,'
Phone Message That Baffles Police

| Officers, However, Argue That Cerulean Citizen Now Is Behind Bars | prowler before he began taking in more territory. Sergt. Patrick Kenealy of the district gave the opinion that the indigo individual was caught in the | Weird Report Received By Woman Promptly Relayed to Headquarters. |

the hand was "large and white," one that was impossible to belong to any "blue man."

In a January 18 news story, a lodger at a nearby boarding house named Virgil Hobbs claimed to have seen the figure on the streets on several occasions. The first time he spotted the Blue Man, a neighbor named Walter Fogel took a shot at it.

"As he shot," Virgil recalled, "I saw a tall figure wearing a black overcoat, and a black soft hat climb over the coal shed at the rear of the Fogel yard and disappear into the night."

Virgil added, "Five minutes later, when a crowd had gathered in front of the house, I saw a man who, as I remember, looked suspiciously like the figure I had just seen to disappear, walking leisurely down Eighth Street. The man stopped and inquired about the excitement and, when told by one of those standing by, laughed and passed on. On the three other occasions that the intruder was scared off, the stranger passed by, and each time the man, who was white and weighed about 180 pounds, wore the same black overcoat and black hat."

Virgil was amazed that the man had so far eluded capture. "He seemed to have no fear as he repeatedly braved the shots of those watching for him." He added that the man seemed very clever, as evidenced by the fact that on the second night of his appearance the Fogel house, the Blue Man was "surrounded by 15 patrolmen, five detectives and two members of the military force," and yet, still gave them the slip.

What made the whole business even stranger is that no one had any idea what the Blue Man wanted or was trying to accomplish with his startling appearances. The police were called again and again to the area around Eighth and Kentucky Streets after sightings were called in to the Sixth Police District Station. They would arrive to find volunteers already searching the area, but whoever - or whatever - the Blue Man was, he always got away. Louisville residents could only speculate that he--or it--had "iron nerve, no brains, or an irresistible desire to obtain possession of a thing, or things unknown."

The mystery continued to be a mystery.

On January 19, the now nightly hunt for the "Blue Man" took an unexpected turn. Two detectives who were keeping watch for the figure at Eighth and Kentucky Streets saw a man named Stewart Graven walking past them carrying a suitcase and a bundle. Suspicious, the police officers followed Graven to his home. After he went inside, the detectives knocked on the door and politely forced their way inside.

The residence, they reported, "looked like a storeroom," filled with expensive goods of all kinds. When questioned, Graven confessed to theft from the American Railway Express Company - and it had been going on for a long time. He told them he was out of work and couldn't let his wife and children starve. He was arrested and charged with grand larceny. A reporter suggested that Graven might be the elusive Blue Man and when he heard this, he laughed. "Me, the Blue Man?" he chuckled. "I wish I was. If I was, I wouldn't be in here right now!"

Meanwhile, the Blue Man kept busy - not committing robberies but scaring the daylights out of downtown residents.

One night, Emma Perkins heard noises outside her home, like the voice of someone talking very low. She investigated but found nothing. The following night, however, she saw someone peering into her window. The face disappeared, and by the time she opened the door, whoever it had been was gone.

'Blue Man'---Clever, Daring Intruder Here---Who Is He?

There Are Many Theories to Account for His Strange Action When Seen Near Eighth and Kentucky Streets, But None of the Theorists Have Caught Him.

Iron nerve, no brains or an irresistible desire to obtain possession of a thing, or things unknown, were theories advanced last night in explanation of the operations of the so-called "blue-man" recently in the vicinity of Eighth and Kentucky Streets.

The mysterious figure apparently has suspended operations in that particular locality, as the last time it was actually seen was about 8:30 o'clock Thursday night according to Mrs. Earl Schubnell, 1013 South Eighth Street.

Mrs. Schubnell said that she was sitting where she could see into the kitchen when she heard the shutter of one of the windows being opened and saw a hand thrust in through the window in which the pane was broken.

"The hand caught hold of the curtain and pulled it back," she said. "but when I screamed, it was withdrawn quickly and I heard the sound of someone running out of the alley and down the street in the direction

tall figure wearing a black overcoat and a black soft hat climb over the coal shed at the rear of the Fogel yard and disappear into the night."

"Five minutes later, when a crowd had gathered in front of the house, I saw a man who, as I remember, looked suspiciously like the figure I had just seen to disappear, walking leisurely down Eighth Street. The man stopped and inquired about the excitement, and when told by one of those standing by, laughed and passed on.

"On the three other occasions that the intruder was scared off," asserted Hobbs, "the stranger passed by, and each time the man, who was white and weighed about 180 pounds, wore the same black overcoat and black hat."

That the intruder had an iron nerve was evidenced according to Hobbs, by the fact that on one occasion he returned to the scene fifteen minutes after he had been shot at by the police who had been summoned.

"He seemed to have no fear," Hobbs said. "as he repeatedly braved the shots of those watching for him. He was clever, too, in evading attempts at his capture, for on the second night

door, whoever it had been was gone.

The next night, someone raised a window in the room of Stewart Friend, a boarder of Mrs. Perkins. He shouted, and the person fled - only to return on January 20. This time, Stewart was ready, and when the window went up, he rushed over with his revolver in hand. A figure was there, just a few feet away, and he raised his gun and fired. He saw "it" fall against the fence. Mrs. Perkins, when she heard the commotion, ran outside with her gun and fired at the intruder. Both were certain that their bullets struck the figure.

Eerily, though, when they examined the scene, they found only a few bullet holes in the fence. The Blue Man was gone. There was no blood or any other trace that he had been there at all.

The following night, the story took another weird turn. Around 9:30 p.m., Henry Etzel was reading the newspaper and heard someone lightly knocking on his front door. This was odd. The gate in front of Henry's South Preston Street home always creaked loudly when it was opened, and he hadn't heard any sound. He checked the door and found no one was there.

Assuming he'd imagined the knocks, he went back to his newspaper. A couple of minutes later, he heard more knocking, louder than before. He jumped from his chair, hurried to the door, and threw it open. Again, no one was outside.

He returned to his newspaper but stayed alert, ready to move even faster if it happened again - and it did. Someone kicked at the door several times. Henry moved so fast that he reached the door before the sound stopped, but there was still no one there.

Outside of the door, though, he found a note lying on the stoop. It read: "I will call again. Don't be afraid. Your friend, the 'Blue Man' till we meet again."

On the night of January 22, Mrs. L.I. Dilly was home alone with her children when an intruder attempted to get into her apartment. The knob clicked back and forth, and weight was applied to the door - she saw it start to give, she later told the police. In a panic, she ran out the side door to the home of her friend and neighbor, Mrs. G.S. Spalding, who was also home alone with her children. Mrs. Spalding had just opened her back door when the two women saw a man jump over the back fence.

They called the police, but when officers arrived, they searched the backyard and found nothing - not even a footprint in the muddy area. They returned to the Sixth District station, but 15 minutes later, they were back at the Dilly home again.

Mrs. Dilly had gone to bed but admitted she had barely closed her eyes before she heard footsteps outside the house.

Again, she heard the doorknob turning and someone pressing against the door. She was too terrified to get out of bed this time.

Soon, the sounds at the door stopped, and she saw a shadow pass by the window. A moment later, a face pressed against the glass.

Her terror now left her, and she grabbed a gun from the nightstand and raced outside. Seeing a figure fleeing across the yard, she raised her weapon and pulled the trigger. The hammer came down with a click. The pistol had refused to fire. By now, the man was gone.

Police officers arrived on the scene, and for the second time that night, they fruitlessly searched the yard for footprints. They wondered if the intruder might be the Blue Man who had been stalking the area, and Mrs. Dilly and Mrs. Spalding admitted they wondered the same thing. The policemen told the women to call again if anything else happened, and they returned to the station.

The officers, Corporal H.C. Griffin and Patrolman E.T. Thornberry, had just started to describe what had happened to other police officers at the station when the telephone rang. A hasty conversation followed, and the men announced they were on their way back to the Dilly home - the Blue Man was back again. They hustled out of the station with two other officers close behind them.

Mrs. Dilly had returned to bed a third time, she later told the officers and was just pulling up the covers around her when she heard a faint noise. She clutched her gun - after making sure it would work this time - and waited for whatever might happen next.

The door was not touched this time, but a shadow flitted across the windowpane a moment before a shadowy face darkened the glass. She ran out to the yard and opened fire at the prowler. This time, she heard a moan of "Oh, oh!"

She'd gotten him this time. The Blue Man had been shot.

Mrs. Dilly and Mrs. Spalding excitedly greeted the police officers when they arrived. She said the Blue Man had been wounded and led the men to the backyard for the third time. Powerful flashlights swept over the yard - and found nothing.

There were no footprints, no blood, not even a bullet hole in the house next door.

The police officers scratched their heads, and the two women looked at each other in confusion. The strange figure has escaped once again.

Early on the morning of January 23, Mrs. J.G. Crider was awakened by her telephone ringing. She groggily reached for the receiver, and when she answered, a husky voice said, "The Blue Man. Last seen Eighth and Walnut!" The line went dead. She called the police, and they investigated but found nothing other than that her telephone was in working order.

On the night of January 29, the Blue Man entertained himself by ringing doorbells. At 9:00 p.m., Mr. and Mrs. E.O. Mershon telephoned the police complaining of hearing "three different kinds of strange noises" around their house. First, the bell was rung several times. That was followed by noises like snow sliding off the roof, "only it wasn't." Mrs. Mershon said that she hadn't noticed any strangers around the neighborhood and that no one had tried to get inside - it was only the noises. The police chalked up another prank by the Blue Man.

A few hours later, another call came in. Mrs. Stanley Searcy reported that her doorbell had been ringing almost continuously from dusk to 11:00 p.m. It was, she said indignantly, the third night in a row she had been pestered with incessant ringing. Although she stood watch from her window, she saw or heard no one - just the ringing.

The police were at a loss as to how to help either of the callers. The Blue Man seemed impossible to catch.

In February, the Blue Man was still around but seemed to have returned to his original stomping grounds around Eighth and Kentucky, revisiting some of those who had encountered him first.

A member of the Fogel family - you'll remember that Walter Fogel was the first person to take a shot at the intruder - was bedridden by illness and was being pestered every night by a face that was pressed against the pane of his window. "It has been shot at, and the bullets struck thin air. When the image appeared, members of the family run to the outside but never have seen anything more than darkness."

When the family consulted a fortune teller, she told them that when the "thing" got what it wanted, it would go away.

What did it want? She couldn't say.

One of the first to report the Blue Man, Reese Carrell, claimed that the Blue Man had been hanging around his home for days. One night, it even crept into the house and stole a pair of trousers. Reese shot at the intruder several times, but the bullets had no effect, just like every other time.

Reese's father tried shooting at the figure. "I never missed a rabbit or a bird in my life," Mr. Carrell complained, "but the shots went right through him." When asked if he thought the intruder was a ghost, Carrell Sr. retorted, "Ghost? What would a ghost want with my pants?"

And soon after that, the Blue Man was gone. He went the way of so many other sinister strangers and just simply vanished to - well, who knows?

The bizarre collection of sightings remains a mystery. Louisville residents never figured out what the Blue Man wanted or what he was up to, and even today, we are just as baffled as they were in 1921.

6. MAD GASSER MANIA

There is no doubt that a gas maniac exists and has made a number of attacks. But many of the reported attacks are nothing more than hysteria. Fear of the gas man is entirely out of proportion to the menace of the relatively harmless gas he is spraying. The whole town is sick with hysteria.

Police Commissioner Thomas V. Wright, Mattoon, Illinois

Speaking for myself, I believe there is no greater "sinister stranger" in the history of the unexplained in America than the legendary "Mad Gasser of Mattoon," a mysterious figure that wreaked havoc in a small Illinois town in 1944.

He turned out to be so elusive that law enforcement officials eventually just declared him nonexistent, despite dozens of eyewitness reports and actual physical evidence that was left behind at the scene of some of the attacks.

I grew up in Central Illinois - many decades after the attacks - but I was fascinated by what had happened during these incidents because Mattoon was barely an hour from where I lived and where my parents still live today. Honestly, if not for the "Mad Gasser," this book would not be in your hands today. I could never get enough of the story, and I've written about it many times over the years, although none of those accounts were as complete as the one that follows.

It would be years later when I discovered that Mattoon's Gasser was not the only "Anesthetic Prowler" in America's history. A series of nearly identical attacks took place in Botetourt County, Virginia, in 1933 and 1934. Social scientists later declared that the attacks in Mattoon had been nothing more than mass hysteria, but how could the Illinois residents have known anything about the events in Virginia, which were barely publicized, to duplicate them so closely?

Both series of attacks involved a mysterious figure, dressed in black, who came and went without warning, left little in the way of clues behind, and for some reason, sprayed a paralyzing gas into the windows of unsuspecting residents. The gas was never identified in either incident, and the attacks in both places occurred in fairly isolated places. The homes that were attacked in Virginia were in a rural county, and Mattoon, at that time, was a small, Central Illinois town with no large cities in the vicinity. Also, police officials were totally stumped in both Virginia and Illinois.

But what really makes the mystery so compelling is that the central figure in both places remains such a mystery.

Who -- or what -- attacked the unsuspecting citizens of Virginia and Illinois? Was it a mad scientist carrying out some secret experiments? A government agency? A visitor from another planet? No one will ever know for sure, as you have discovered in the preceding pages, inexplicable attackers who appear and vanish without explanation, prey on the unsuspecting without warning, and then vanish completely, leaving no trace behind are not as uncommon as we might wish they were.

THE BOTETOURT GASSER

In 1933, Botetourt County, in the southwest part of Virginia, was a quiet area of the state and had never really experienced much out of the ordinary.

That all began to change on December 22, when the home of Mr. and Mrs. Cal Huffman, near Haymakertown, was attacked by a mysterious figure that was unlike anything seen, or even heard of, in the region before.

Around 10:00 that evening, Mrs. Huffman was preparing for bed and noticed a strange odor. Almost immediately, she became nauseated and alerted her husband. They could find no source for the smell, but as Mrs. Huffman's illness passed, she decided to go to bed.

Cal, suspicious about where the odor had come from, decided to stay up for a little while. He worried that someone might be on the property.

A half-hour later, another wave of the strange smell spread through the room. Cal was convinced that it was some sort of gas - like that used on soldiers who fought in World War I. He grabbed his shotgun and ran outside, but no one was there. He decided to call the police and ran to the nearby home of his landlord, K.W. Henderson and used his telephone.

A call was made to the sheriff's department and Officer O.D. Lemon was dispatched to the scene. He listened carefully to the story told by the Huffmans. He could tell they were frightened and offered to stay with them for a while in case whoever had sprayed the gas returned. He stayed around until nearly midnight and then departed, telling them that he would return if there were any further problems.

Officer Lemon's car had just left the driveway when the attacker struck again. The third wave of gas filled both floors of the house. All eight members of the Huffman family, along with Ashby Henderson, were affected by the gas. Ashby and Cal Huffman had been keeping watch for the return of the prowler and thought that they saw a man running away after the attack.

According to reports, the gas caused the victims to become very nauseous, gave them a headache, and caused the mouth and throat muscles to restrict. Their eyes and throats burned as they coughed and gasped for air.

Alice, the Huffmans' 19-year-old daughter, was overwhelmed by the gas and had to be given artificial respiration to revive her. She was said to have experienced convulsions for some time afterward. Her doctor, Dr. S.F. Driver, later reported that while part of her condition was caused by extreme nervousness over the attack, he had no doubt that the gas attack was responsible for the fact that her condition continued.

However, no one could determine what kind of gas was used or how it was sprayed into the house. Dr. W.N. Breckinridge, who assisted with the police investigation, ruled out ether, chloroform, and tear gas.

The greater mystery was who had done it - and why? Cal Huffman seemed to have no enemies, and neither did anyone else in the family. The only clue that Officer Lemon found at the scene was the print of a woman's shoe beneath the window into which the attacker was thought to have sprayed his gas.

The Huffmans recovered quickly. The story was given little attention in the local newspaper, and few people noticed it anyway. It was too close to Christmas, and minds were elsewhere at that time of year. Besides, there was no reason to think it had been anything but an isolated incident. No one had ever heard of an intruder who sprayed toxic gas into random homes. It was unlikely it would ever happen again.

And then it did.

The Botetourt County community of Cloverdale was a little south of Haymakertown, and on the night of December 24, Clarence Hall, his wife, and their two children arrived home from a church service around 9:00 p.m. As soon as they walked in the front door, they noticed a strange and very strong odor in the house. The smell seemed to be coming from one of the back rooms of the house, and Clarence went to investigate. He came back moments later, staggering and swaying. His wife, who also felt nauseous and weak, had to drag him outside to the porch. The entire family was left terrified and gasping for air in the front yard.

Fortunately, Mrs. Hall's mother lived nearby, and the family decided it would be best to stay there for the night. The effects of the gas did not linger with Clarence, but Mrs. Hall experienced eye irritation for the next two days.

When sheriff's deputies arrived, they entered the Hall house to look around. Dr. Breckinridge again helped the police, and he noted that the gas "tasted sweet" and that he detected a trace of formaldehyde in it. He still had no idea what the gas was, though, and investigators again found only one clue at the scene. Near the front of the house, they found a window that had previously been nailed shut. Apparently, one of the nails had been pulled from the windows. Was this to make it possible to spray the gas inside?

After their harrowing night, the family decided to return home the following day to celebrate Christmas. They spent the day together, but as darkness approached, Mrs. Hall began to worry that the attacker might return. She decided it would be best to take the children back to their grandmother's house and for the family to spend another night there.

Later that evening, around 8:00, Mrs. Hall's sister and her husband drove up to the empty house. They had stopped by to check on them and, ironically, to try to convince them to return to their mother's home for the night. They parked in front and tapped on the horn, and at that moment, they saw a light appear on the side of the house - the same side where investigators had found the window with the missing nail. Afraid to confront a stranger in the dark, they quickly drove away.

On December 27, another gas attack occurred. This one happened at the home of a welder named A.L. Kelly, who lived with his mother in Troutville. Oddly, the police learned that a man and a woman in a 1933 Chevrolet had been seen driving back and forth in front of Kelly's house around the time of the attack. A neighbor managed to get a partial plate number on the car, but the police were unable to locate it.

No attacks took place over the next two weeks, but on January 10, 1934, the Gasser struck again at the home of Homer Hylton, near Haymakertown.

Hylton and his wife were upstairs asleep, and their daughter, Mrs. Moore, whose husband was out of town on business, was sleeping downstairs. Around 10:00, she got up to attend to her baby and later recalled hearing mumbling voices outside and someone fiddling with the window. That particular window had been cracked some time ago, and a small piece of glass was missing from one corner. To keep out cold drafts, a rag had been stuffed into the corner, and the window shade was pulled down.

As Mrs. Moore watched intently, she saw the shade move, as though someone was pushing it from outside. Moments later, she said that the room filled with gas, and as she grabbed her child, she experienced a "marked feeling of numbness." Regardless, she managed to run screaming from the room, alerting her parents.

When sheriff's deputies arrived, they interviewed the family, and as in the previous attacks, the Hyltons claimed to have no enemies and had no idea why anyone would want to attack them. Investigators had also not found any connection between the families who had been attacked, which seemed to rule out revenge.

The Gasser just seemed to be choosing houses at random, which made his actions even more terrifying.

A neighbor of the Hyltons, G.K. Poague, told the police that he suspected his house had also been targeted that night. Although no attack had occurred, Poague reported hearing the same muffled voices that Mrs. Moore had been bothered by around that same time.

However, another house, owned by G.D. Kinzie, was attacked in Troutville that night. This case was not reported until later and was different from the others. Dr. S.F. Driver, who was also assisting the police, stated that he believed the gas used in the attack was chlorine. Chlorine was then mentioned in several subsequent accounts until a Roanoke chemistry professor later ruled it out as a possible cause.

After a few quiet nights, the Gasser returned on January 16, this time attacking the home of F.B. Duval near Bonsack. Duval left the house to summon the police and, as he reached a nearby intersection, saw a man run up to a parked car and speed away. He and Officer Lemon spent several hours driving around searching for the car, but they found nothing. The next day, Lemon again found the prints of a woman's shoes, this time where the car had been parked.

On January 19, 1934, the Gasser struck again.

On January 19, the Gasser struck again. This time, gas was sprayed into the window of a Mrs. Campbell, a former magistrate's wife, at Carvin's Cove, near Cloverdale. She was sitting near the window in question and became sick moments after seeing the shade move.

This time, the authorities were ready and tried to trap the attacker by cutting off the only routes in and out of Carvin's Cove, a quiet, isolated settlement about eight miles outside of Roanoke. Several local officers, including Officer Lemon, joined the Roanoke County Sheriff George Richardson to set up roadblocks and catch the Gasser.

It didn't work.

At some point in the night, he managed to escape Carvin's Cove and left very little evidence behind for investigators to find. The press called the Gasser "ghostly," which was as good a word as any to describe him.

A few nights later, the gas attacks reached their peak, with five attacks taking place over a period of three nights.

The first attack took place on January 21 when Howard Crawford and his wife returned to their home between Cloverdale and Troutville. Mr. Crawford went into the house first to light a lamp but quickly stumbled back out. He was overwhelmed by the gas and staggered to the home of a neighbor, Kent Scaggs, to ask for help.

Ken went to the nearest telephone to call the police. Soon, Officer Lemon, Sheriff Zimmerman, and Dr. Driver were at the scene. The doctor again suggested chlorine gas was used in the attack but couldn't be sure. Ken Scaggs was interviewed, and he told the two lawmen that when he was on his way to the closest telephone, he had passed an automobile on the road that drove past him without its headlights on.

The investigators were again able to find only a single clue at the house -- the crank of an old automobile. The metal crank seemed to have absolutely nothing to do with the attack, but it was simply too strange of an item to be left behind. On the other hand, it was also too common of an item in those days to be traced.

On January 22, three separate attacks occurred in Carvin's Cove. In just one hour, the Gasser covered about two miles, attacking in order moving southward, the homes of Ed Reedy, George C. Riley, and Raymond Etter. At each of the houses, the victims all claimed to have numbness and nausea. Riley called his brother, a Roanoke police officer, and a blockade of the nearby roads was quickly put into place. Although the Gasser managed to elude the authorities again, one of Mr. Etter's sons claimed to see a figure disappearing from the direction of the house. He gave chase and even fired a few shots at the man from about 30 yards, but Gasser got away.

On January 23, Mrs. R.H. Hartsell and her family spent the night with some neighbors, and when they returned to their Pleasantdale Church home at 4:30 a.m., they discovered that the house had been filled with gas. For some bizarre reason, someone had also piled wood and brush against their front door during the night. The only possible motive that I can see for this would have been to keep the family from easily escaping once the house was filled with gas. This means that the elusive Gasser must have believed the family was home at the time of the attack.

This new series of gassings had the entire community in an uproar. Families who lived in more isolated areas began spending the night with friends and neighbors, hoping to find security in numbers. Local men began patrolling the roadways at night, armed with shotguns and rifles. The local newspaper, the

Roanoke Times, stated that it was sure the gassers would be caught, and it pleaded with the farmers not to shoot anyone.

The authorities were now growing more concerned. Prior to this, they had believed the gassings had been nothing more than pranks played by some mischievous boys. Now the county sheriff's office was forced to admit that if this had been the case, the boys would have been caught long before. They had begun to investigate the idea that a mentally deranged person might be the culprit, perhaps even an unhinged gas victim from World War I.

On January 25, the Gasser may have attempted to strike again, but this time was foiled. Chester Snyder had been entertaining visitors at his home near Cloverdale that evening, and after they left, he received a call from one of his guests, Lindell Newman. According to Lindell, as he was leaving, he had spotted a suspicious-looking man on the road about a half-mile from Chester's house.

An undercurrent of fear was running through the whole county now, and neighbors were on alert, looking out for each other.

Chester went to bed early that night, and at about 9:00, he was awakened by the sound of his dog barking. Chester, likely thinking about the call from his friend, jumped out of bed and dashed downstairs. He grabbed his shotgun from the closet and darted outside. Chester ran across the yard and fired a shot at a man he saw "creeping along a ditch" about 20 feet from the house. Apparently, though, the shot went wide, and Snyder only had one shell in his gun. He ran back inside for more ammunition, but by the time he returned, the man was gone.

He called the police. Sherriff Zimmerman came to investigate the scene. He managed to find footprints that led from the road to the ditch and signs that the prowler had hidden behind a tree on the property for some time before the dog sounded the alarm. More tracks led from the tree to the house and then stopped, marking the point where the man had retreated.

There was, of course, no real evidence to say that the prowler was the Gasser, but based on the events that had been occurring, any sort of incident like this was immediately suspect.

On January 28, the Gasser did manage to pull off an attack in Cloverdale, and he would later return to this same residence and attack again. The home belonged to Ed Stanley, and Ed, his wife, and three other adults - Franky Guy, Dorothy Garrett, and Mrs. Henry Weddle -- were all affected by the still mysterious gas. The men choked and gasped, but the women were more severely sickened. Mrs. Weddle even had to be carried out of the house.

Frank, who worked as a hired hand on the Stanley farm, ran outside immediately after the gas filled the house and said he saw four men running into the woods near the farm. He ran back inside to get his gun, and when he returned to the yard, he couldn't see the fleeing figures but could hear them in the woods. He fired several shots in the direction of the voices but felt that it was unlikely that he hit anything.

The Gasser returned two nights later and attempted to attack the Stanley House again. This time, however, Ed heard a sound outside the window before the attack took place. What happened after that remains a mystery as no further details were reported.

The last of the likely authentic gas attacks took place in Nace, two miles from Troutville, on February 3. The house that was attacked belonged to A.P. Scaggs. He and his wife and five other adults were all affected by the gas. The group was so severely hurt by the gas that Sheriff Williamson would tell the skeptics who later emerged to question the gassing cases, "No amount of imagination in the world would make people as ill as the Skaggs are."

The attack became as dramatic as the first attack on the Huffman family, and it's been noted that perhaps the Gasser wanted to mark his entrance and exit with large attacks.

Another similarity to the Huffman attack was that it seemed as though the gas was sprayed into the house two times that evening, although Officer Lemon stated that he believed lingering gas near the ceiling could have been responsible for what seemed to be a separate attack.

Oddly, after the attack, but before any curious neighbors arrived, Scaggs reportedly saw "a light similar to a flashlight" outside the house. This sounds a lot like the light seen outside the Hall house after the attack.

The gas had some strange effects on the people in the house. On the night of the attack, after Officer Lemon had arrived, one of Scaggs' nephews was alone in a room. Suddenly, he shouted "Gas!" and ran out of the room. But instead of going outside, he ran into an adjoining room and began screaming hysterically that he was "trapped" in the house. Although this sounds like panic, the nephew insisted that he was not easily scared and that the gas had done something very strange to him.

The gas also seemed to affect the family dog, ruling out the idea that the attack was hysteria or wild imagination. Officer

Lemon returned to the house to continue his investigation the next day, and one of the children came in crying that the dog was dying. Lemon went out and saw that the animal was rolling over and over in the snow, just as dogs do when a skunk sprays them. As no skunk odor was present, this certainly seemed odd. The well-trained dog was sick and would not pay attention to commands for some time after the incident.

That was not the end of the alleged attacks, but it became hard to take them very seriously after that.

During the following week, there were 20 attacks reported in Roanoke County and several reports in Lexington, about 30 miles away.

In Vinton, Mrs. Bohon and her daughter, Beverly, were in their living room with Mrs. Bohon's sister when they noticed a strange odor and felt sick.

At the same time, a neighbor, Mrs. Cage, claimed that someone sprayed gas under her front door while she was bathing her children in an upstairs bathroom.

A few blocks away, Mrs. Milan claimed she was lying on the living room floor with her daughter, and they noticed a strange smell coming from the front door. A neighbor came over and also smelled the odor. Mrs. Milan decided that it seemed stronger near the carpet in front of the door, so she dragged it out on the porch. Leaving the door open to ventilate the house, she telephoned the police and her husband, who was at work.

When Detective W.C. Tate and Sheriff Richardson arrived, they also noticed the smell. A neighbor reported seeing a large car that evening, slowly driving down the street with its headlights off, around the time the gas was detected.

Soon after the police arrived, Mrs. Milan began experiencing chest pains, and a doctor was called. He administered oxygen and ruled out just about any kind of gas that he'd ever seen before. He did not, however, rule out a panic attack.

More gassing incidents were reported from Raleigh Court, Virginia Heights, and neighborhoods all over Roanoke. A Mrs. Langford in Garden City fell ill after an alleged attack at her home on February 8. Officers were unable to find any strange odors in the house.

That same night, a health department employee, J.F. Clay, called the police to his home and stated that one of his children had fallen ill after smelling a strange odor. No one else in the house was affected, and the officers who responded didn't smell anything out of the ordinary.

Another call came in from the Wade family in Roanoke. Joe Wade told police that he heard the door on his back porch open and then slam shut. When he went into the kitchen at the rear of the house to investigate, the air was heavy with noxious gas. He ran to a nearby drug store and telephoned for help. When officers arrived at the house, they admitted they did smell something but could not identify it.

And there were more - a lot more. In one report, a maid called the police after seeing a strange vehicle stop in front of the house where she worked. Another caller reported a stranger had walked up on her porch late at night before driving away in a car that had been left running at the curb.

The Patterson family called the police after a suspected gas attack. Officers who responded couldn't detect any unusual smells and found no evidence of a prowler, so they left. As they were driving away, a panicked Mrs. Patterson called again to say the smell had returned. Again, the officers searched the home and found nothing.

For days, calls flooded the Roanoke police switchboard reporting mysterious vapors, and the stories of the "attacks" were dutifully reported in the newspaper, further stoking the panic. Beginning each evening just after sunset, police officers were kept busy chasing the Gasser all over the city until nearly midnight. There turned out to be no valid reports of any kind and not even a hint of nauseating gas. Most cases were easily dismissed as overreactions to common smells like car exhaust, coal stoves, radiators, and even a shoe that was placed too close to a fireplace.

Hysteria had fully gripped the city, but police officers responded to each and every call. Some of these men had been involved in the investigations into the earlier attacks and knew those had been genuine. The cases they were seeing now lacked the detail of the original incidents and were linked to ordinary odors and pranksters.

Finally, on February 18, the newspaper published an article declaring that the police now believed the Gasser - at least as far as the attacks in Roanoke were concerned - to be a product of mass hysteria. After 19 reports and not a single sighting of a perpetrator and no physical evidence left behind, they had determined the panic in the city to be unjustified. The public was implored to calm down before things got out of hand.

And then, as quickly as he had arrived, the Gas vanished from the newspaper headlines. Though it likely took a little longer for calls reporting suspicious odors to stop coming into the police department, it became clear that the newspaper article would be the final word on the subject.

The cases in Roanoke had begun just about the time that the cases in Botetourt County - the legitimate cases, in my opinion - had ended. That was when I believe the Gasser actually ended his attacks. Although why he stopped spraying gas into houses remains as baffling as to why he had started doing it in the first place, but we'll never know the answer to that.

For many, it was easy to write off *all* the incidents to mass hysteria and panic after it became clear that the "attacks" in

Roanoke were imaginations and fear at work. The public was quick to accept the idea that the gas attacks had been nothing more than faulty chimney flues, gas leaks, and hysteria. It made more sense and didn't require a belief in a sinister prowler who sprayed gas into windows and escaped without getting caught.

Those who were attacked and the authorities that investigated those original attacks - like Officer Lemon and Sheriff Richardson - never accepted "mass hysteria" explanation for what they had encountered. But the cases in Roanoke didn't win over any skeptics to the idea that any of the attacks were real.

In hindsight, though, when we compare the incidents in Botetourt County to the incidents in Roanoke, the later cases actually help make the original attacks more convincing. The Roanoke cases didn't follow the pattern of the original attacks; they occurred outside of the already established area, occurred at no particular times, and did not cause any lasting effects. In addition, the original attacks were spread out over such a wide area that neighbors were unable to infect one another with hysteria, as they were about to do in Roanoke.

If mass hysteria was not to blame for the Botetourt County attacks, is there another plausible explanation besides a Mad Gasser?

Was there something man-made at work? Could this have been some sort of natural gas in the homes? Since most houses in Botetourt County in the 1930s had wood or coal heat, it would have had to have been fumes from something in the furnace or woodstove, but there was never any evidence of that. There was little pollution in the area and not all the houses had chimney flues, so that explanation doesn't really work either, especially when we examine the various elements of each incident - the selection of victims, times of the evening when attacks took place, intense police investigations, and, of course, the fleeing figure or figures that were seen running away from the residences where attacks occurred.

So, if there were people involved in the incidents, could they have been hoaxes instead of actual gas attacks? There is no evidence to suggest this, even though it was rare to find evidence left behind by a lone attacker. Botetourt County wasn't an overly populated place in the 1930s, and the police officers who investigated the incidents were acquainted with just about everyone. There was never any discussion about the victims faking the attacks or their reactions to them. As Sheriff Williamson said about the Skaggs family, no amount of imagination could explain how sick they were from the gas.

If pressed for an answer, I would have to say that I believe the Gasser of Botetourt County cases were real. Someone - or something - attacked those families, left no useful clues behind, and escaped without being captured or identified.

As we have seen with other types of incidents in this book - from Black Ghosts to Killer Clowns - many of these events begin with a few legitimate sightings of *something* and, before long, panic and terror sets in and mistaken encounters with other things blow the story out of proportion. I think that's exactly what happened in Roanoke.

Whoever - or whatever - the Gasser was, he left Virginia in early 1934 and vanished without a trace. He never came back - well, not to Virginia anyway.

But it is possible that he showed up somewhere else a decade after he left Botetourt County. The Mad Gasser - or someone almost exactly like him - arrived to wreak havoc on a small town in Illinois in the fall of 1944.

THE MAD GASSER OF MATTOON

Mattoon, located in the southeastern part of Central Illinois, is a typical Midwestern town. However, the strange events that took place there in 1944 were anything but typical. They placed the small city under the scrutiny of the entire country for just over two weeks and were eventually used against the residents by psychologists and authorities as a textbook case of mass hysteria.

But was it really?

I don't think so. And if you have been paying attention throughout this book, I don't think you'll believe that either. Something did happen in Mattoon, Illinois, in 1944, and it left an edible mark on our history that we should never forget.

The bizarre series of incidents began in the early morning hours of August 31, 1944. Urban Raef was startled out of a deep sleep in his Grant Avenue home and complained to his wife that he felt sick. He questioned her about leaving the stove on in the kitchen because his symptoms seemed very similar to gas exposure. Mrs. Raef started to get out of bed to check the pilot light on the stove but found, to her surprise, that she was unable to move.

Just minutes later, reports state that a woman in a neighboring home also tried to get out of bed and discovered that she was also paralyzed. The effects of whatever had occurred wore off in a few minutes.

On the night of September 1, Mrs. Aline Kearney was home with two daughters, Dorothy and Carol Anne, her sister, Martha, and Martha's little boy, Roger, while her husband, Bert, was at work, driving a cab.

Aline was in her bedroom with Dorothy, the oldest of her girls when she noticed a peculiar smell coming from the open window. The odor was sweet and overpowering, and as it grew stronger, she began to choke and then felt a strange prickling feeling in her legs and lower body. She tried to get up from the bed, but she couldn't move.

Aline screamed for her sister, and Martha burst through the bedroom door. She gagged on the sweet stench that filled the room. When she realized her sister couldn't move, she scooped up Dorothy and took her to the living room. When she laid her down on the couch, Dorothy woke up, confused about what was happening, and started to vomit.

Confused, Martha failed to use the telephone. Instead, she ran next door to the neighbors' house. The Robertsons, already awakened by the screams, ran outside. Martha tried to explain what had happened while Mrs. Robertson called the police.

Mr. Robertson ran into the Kearney house to check on Aline, who was starting to recover. He was still with her when the police arrived a few minutes later. They searched around the house and yard but were unable to find any sign of a prowler.

After answering questions from the police, Aline tried to settle herself back into bed. Dorothy had stopped throwing up, although her feeling of weakness and nausea would last until the following morning. Aline had gotten the worst of the gas. Her paralysis soon faded, but she would later complain of burned lips and a parched mouth and throat from exposure to the gas.

By 11:45, the search by the police officers - and the Kearneys' shaken neighbors - would be called off. The police left the house with instructions to call if anything else strange occurred.

And it would.

Around 12:30 a.m., Bert Kearney arrived home. He had been working the overnight shift but had gotten word that some kind of incident had occurred at his house. Worried, he hurried home to make sure his wife and children were safe.

As Bert turned into the driveway, his headlights swept over the side of the house, and they caught a figure standing outside one of the windows. He quickly parked and jumped out of his cab.

Bert called out loudly and started to run toward the figure, who suddenly turned, aware that he had been spotted. As Bert later described him, the man was very tall, dressed in black, form-fitting clothing, and wearing a tight, black cap on his head. He had been standing outside the same window through which Aline reported the gas had been sprayed less than two hours earlier.

The tall man started to run, and the prowler's long legs quickly outpaced the stride of Bert Kearney, and he vanished into the darkness. Bert broke off the chase and ran back to his house.

When he got inside, he found that no one was hurt, but all of them were frightened. Bert suggested that they pack some things to go and spend the night at an aunt's house on the other side of town.

He was convinced they would be safe there.

But he was wrong. For the next two weeks, no one in Mattoon was really safe.

The events that took place at the Kearny house soon became public knowledge and were widely reported in the local newspaper. At this point, the newspaper was reporting the story as nothing more than an unusual break-in attempt. A prowler had used some sort of knockout gas so that he could make sure everyone was asleep in the house when he broke in to rob it.

But newspaper coverage was soon going to change.

On the morning of Tuesday, September 5, Mattoon residents woke to discover that the Kearneys had not been the first victims of what the newspaper was now calling the "anesthetic prowler."

In addition to the gas leak incident at the Urban Raef home, there was also a report that was at least a month old from Mrs. Olive Brown. She stated that she had not talked about her experience when it happened because it seemed so fantastic. After seeing the story about the Kearney incident, she came forward and related that she and her daughter had gone to bed in separate rooms one night over the summer. Both had also awakened feeling sick and paralyzed from some sort of gas that had been sprayed into their windows. Had the prowler been practicing before starting the series of attacks?

The newspaper story also revealed another attack that had taken place on the night of September 1 - actually in the early morning hours of September 2 - not long after Bert Kearney had chased the man in black away from his bedroom window.

The home of the Rider family was located on Prairie Avenue. Mrs. Rider was home alone with her two children, Ann Marie and Joe, while her husband, George, was at work. When George returned home very early in the morning, she told him of noticing a peculiar odor in the bedroom and that the children were very restless from it. Mrs. Rider said that the fumes did not smell like chloroform but that she was "light-headed" after smelling them.

A short distance west of the Rider home, an unnamed woman and several children also became ill from fumes that had been forced into a bedroom window by the "prowler." The woman had been awakened by the sickly-sweet odor and found her children were crying and vomiting.

Interestingly, the details about each of these incidents were eerily similar, even though none of the witnesses had compared notes or had time to check their stories. There had been very little coverage in the newspaper at that point, and subsequent reports would be nearly identical. In each case, the victims complained of a sickeningly sweet odor that caused them to become sick and slightly paralyzed for up to 30 minutes at a time.

It was also interesting to note that there had been two reports of prowlers in the southwest part of Mattoon over the weekend, and each time, the man had independently been reported the same way - tall, thin, dressed all in black, and wearing a tight black cap on his head.

It was exactly the same way that Bert Kearney had described the "anesthetic prowler."

Late on the night of September 5, the first real clue in the Mattoon Gasser case was discovered. It was found at the home of Carl and Beulah Cordes, who returned to their home on North 21st Street that evening to see a white cloth lying on their front porch. It was not a handkerchief, as has often been reported, but an empty white five-pound salt bag.

Beulah picked it up and noticed that it was giving off a strange smell, like medicine mixed with gardenias. She held it close to her nose and immediately felt nauseated and light-headed. She nearly fainted, and her husband had to help her inside the house. Within minutes, she was seized with a severe allergic reaction. Her lips and face began to swell, and her mouth began to bleed. It would be more than two terrifying hours before the symptoms began to subside.

Carl called the police, and officers came to investigate. They took the cloth bag into evidence and surmised that it might have something to do with the other attacks, even though whatever was on it caused different symptoms in Beulah than in the other victims. She did become sick to her stomach, but there were no sensations of paralysis.

Even so, investigators believed that the Gasser had been trying to break into their house and had been frightened away when the couple came home. If true, it would have meant a change in the pattern because, so far, he had never tried to gain access to any of the homes.

After this attack, Police Chief E.E. Cole ordered his 10-man force on 24-hour duty, and Police Commissioner Thomas V. Wright appealed to the Illinois State Department of Public Safety to send investigators to Mattoon. The cloth from the Cordes' home was sent to state chemists for analysis.

As the newspaper noted, "Police turned to science to determine whether the phantom is a real boogie man who paralyzes his victims with the chemical, or whether he is merely the product of overworked imaginations as a result of too many comic books." Since most of the victims so far had been adult

"ANESTHETIC PROWLER" COVERS CITY

The scope of activities of Mattoon's "anesthetic prowler" ranges across the entire city, it was disclosed today as four more cases including one several months old, were brought to light.

Latest victims were Mr. and Mrs. Urban Raef, 1817 Grant avenue, Mrs. George Rider and children, Ann Marie and Joe, 2508 Prairie avenue, and a woman and children, residing a few blocks from the Rider home, whose names were not revealed. The case which occurred several months ago was at the home of Mrs. Olive Brown and her daughter, Miss Orissie, 208 North Twenty-second street.

The Raef home was the scene of the prowler's activities last Thursday night, the night prior to his appearance at the Bert Kearney residence, 1408 Marshall avenue.

Mr. Raef said today that he and his wife were made sick by the fumes which apparently poured through a bedroom window at their home. He said he awoke about 3 o'clock in the morning and felt ill and as if he were paralyzed.

"There was peculiar heavy odor in the bedroom and I at first thought it was gas," Mr. Raef said. "I asked my wife if she had left the gas stove turned on, but she hadn't. We both had the same feeling of paralysis and were ill for approxi-

women with families, it seems unlikely that "too many comic books" really figured into the incidents.

But if so, then it must have been a pretty sinister "comic book" that sprayed gas into the window of Mrs. Leonard Burrell that night. She awoke "choking and strangling" at about 11:15 p.m. as the mysterious vapor filled her bedroom. Her 18-month-old son, Dennis, who was asleep in another bedroom, was unaffected by the gas.

On September 6, two more gas attacks occurred in Mattoon, despite the watchful eyes of the harried police force, which wasn't equipped to handle mysterious crimes where no clues were left behind. By this time, local volunteers had swelled the ranks of the nightly patrols, but that wasn't enough to keep the Gasser away.

The first took place at the home of Mrs. Ardell Spangler, who lived on North 15th Street and worked at the Brown Shoe Company factory. She was stricken by "sickly sweet fumes" in her bedroom at about 10:00

p.m. that night. She became sick to her stomach and suffered from parched lips and throat but recovered by morning.

The second attack occurred just a few minutes after midnight. Laura Junken was the manager of the Big Four Restaurant on Richmond Avenue and lived in a small apartment at the rear of the café. She had just gone to bed when something she described as smelling like "cheap perfume" was sprayed through an open window. Like many of the other victims, the gas paralyzed her legs for a short time, and were still feeling weak the next day.

Meanwhile, reports of prowlers were still coming in from all over the city, including two from within a block of the Bert Kearney house, where the earlier attack occurred. Each time, these fleeting glimpses of the Gasser always described him as a tall, thin man in black clothing and a tight black cap.

Chief Cole said that many of the calls were probably prompted by "nerves," but, at this point, the authorities were still taking things seriously. Cole spent many nights at police headquarters, personally directing the investigation, but he knew he was out of his depth and anxious for state investigators to arrive.

He was especially anxious after a woman named Mae Williams notified the police that a tall, dark man who fit the Gasser's description had attempted to force her door open, but her screams scared him away.

Rumors were rapidly spreading around the city about the attacks, and there was no shortage of theories about who the Gasser might be. Some of them, based on the senselessness of the whole affair, revolved around the idea that the Gasser was an escapee from an insane asylum. State's Attorney W.K. Kidwell even checked with Illinois mental hospitals for information on men who had recently been released.

Police Commissioner Wright suggested that the Gasser might be an "eccentric inventor" who was testing out a spraying apparatus or a teenager who was experimenting with a chemistry set. Others claimed he was a German spy who was testing out some sort of poisonous gas.

The rumors did nothing to calm residents' fears.

One night, the Gasser indirectly claimed a victim, Hiram Weaver, who suffered a fractured left hip as he searched the Lafayette Avenue home of the McMurray family for the Gasser.

His daughter had been to his house for a visit, and then he walked her back to the McMurray home, where she worked. It was dark by the time they arrived, so Weaver decided to search the property and ensure it was safe. While doing so, he fell into the open stairway of an outside cellar entrance, shattering his hip bone so badly that he needed surgery.

But at least the Gasser wasn't there.

On September 8, it was revealed there were more victims of gas attacks than the police department was admitting. The previous morning, they had denied any new incidents, but Chief Cole admitted the new reports later in the afternoon.

A foundry worker named Fred Goble woke up on the night of September 6, violently ill from a "sweet, sickening" gas. He felt waves of severe nausea pass over him, but his wife, who was sleeping farther away from the open window, suffered no ill effects. At the same time as the attack, a neighbor named Daniels reported seeing a "tall man" fleeing between their two houses.

Other victims whose stories were not immediately released included an 11-year-old girl named Glenda Hendershott, who was overwhelmed by gas at her family's home on South 14th Street; Daniel Spohn, who lived on North 19th Street; and Mrs. Cordie Taylor, who was attacked in her home on Charleston

Avenue. There is little detail offered about any of these incidents - only that they were nauseated and partially paralyzed by a sweet-smelling gas that was sprayed into their windows. Like other victims, they also suffered burned mouths and throats, and their faces became swollen, as if from an allergic reaction.

Others added to the "Mad Man's List" were Miss Frances Smith, the principal of the Columbian Grade School, and her sister, Maxine. Incredibly, they claimed to have been attacked four different times - once on Wednesday night and three on Thursday night. They were overwhelmed with the gas each time and became sick. They awoke to a "gassy odor" and then began choking and felt their arms and legs go numb.

They also said that as the sweet odor began to fill the room "as a thin, blue vapor." They heard a buzzing noise from outside and believed that the Gasser's "spraying apparatus" was in operation.

Earlier on Thursday evening, a cab driver had noticed a strange odor outside of the C.W. Driskell home on DeWitt Avenue and reported it to the police. It was suggested that perhaps it had been the Gasser, and he was frightened away by the cab.

If it was, though, he came back.

Later that night, Mrs. Violet Driskell and her 11-year-old daughter, Ramona, were sleeping when they were awakened by the sound of someone opening a window in the bedroom. They hurried out of bed and tried to run outside for help, but the fumes overcame Ramona, and she began throwing up. When Violet made it out onto the porch, she called for help and believed that she saw a man running away from the house.

Meanwhile, help was starting to arrive for the overworked and inexperienced police department. Richard T. Piper, superintendent of the State Bureau of Criminal Identification and Investigation out of Springfield, came to Mattoon to offer

MATTOON'S GAS FIEND ATTACKS GIRL, 11, IN HOME

Massmeeting Tomorrow; Civilians Join Search.

BY CHARLES BALLENGER.
[Chicago Tribune Press Service.]

Mattoon, Ill., Sept. 9 [Saturday].—The mysterious night prowler who has terrorized this town for the last week by spraying a sickening "poison gas" thru open bedroom windows was reported to have reappeared last night in the northwest section.

Eleven year old Ramona Driskell fled from her home when she and her mother, Mrs. Violet Driskell, were aroused by a prowler, who, they said, attempted to remove a storm sash from their bedroom window. The girl said the fumes assailed her and made her ill as she stood on the porch, calling for help. Mrs. Driskell said she believed she saw the man run away.

assistance. He told reporters, "This is one of the strangest cases I have encountered in many years of police work."

Piper also admitted that the chemist the state had used to analyze the salt bag found at the Cordes' home was unable to identify any kind of gas. "It makes it more mysterious than ever," Piper said. "The chemist said there wasn't a trace of a chemical in the sack. It had all evaporated. Neither was he able to make anything of a stain found on it."

He added that he believed that whatever gas was being sprayed into windows in town was "homemade." The chemists didn't believe that it was chloroform, although it had some of the same properties. It also shared some traits with a poison called chloropicrin, which was used to kill rats and vermin.

Armed Mattoon residents decided on their own that the police needed help and took to the streets, organizing watchers and patrols to try and stop further attacks. Rumors spread that the Gasser had left behind footprints at the scene of some attacks and had sliced open window screens at others. If true, this meant he was just an ordinary man and could be caught.

A citizen's vigilance committee - which had once been the Anti-Horse Thief Association -- did manage to arrest one suspect, but after he passed a polygraph test, he was released.

Local businessmen announced that they would be holding a mass protest rally on Saturday, September 10, to put more pressure on the already pressured Mattoon police force. The Gasser had become more than a threat to public safety. He was now a political liability and a blot of Mattoon's public image.

But the Gasser - whoever he was - didn't care. He continued his attacks.

On September 9, he sprayed his mysterious fumes into the partially opened window of a room where Mrs. Russell Bailey, Katherine Tuzzo, Mrs. Genevieve Haskell, and her eight-year-old son, Grayson, were sleeping.

Genevieve and Grayson, who were guests of Mrs. Bailey, packed up and left town the next day.

The next night, Mrs. Lucy Stephens and her nine-year-old nephew, Jimmy Harden, were awakened coughing and choking from fumes that had been sprayed into their window. They had been sleeping in a first-floor bedroom at the Harden home on North 32nd Street and didn't see the Gasser after he struck.

Mrs. George Hampton, who lived on Champaign Avenue, was rushed to the hospital that same night after inhaling fumes that had been forced through a window.

Mr. and Mrs. Carl Grisamore were also attacked in their home that night. They fled from the bedroom as gas entered their home on Charleston Avenue.

By now, the town was beside itself with fear. State agents - including Piper and Francis Berry -- had arrived to lend a hand, and State Police Chief Harry Yde ordered ten state patrolmen to Mattoon to aid officers in policing the town. Investigators weren't just trying to track down the Gasser but were also trying to keep armed civilians off the streets. They had managed to talk the organizers out of the mass protest that had been planned, getting them to agree that it would serve no purpose other than to increase the panic in the community.

But even without the protest, people were terrified.

Many people, especially parents with small children, were fleeing the city to escape the Gasser. Others were sitting up all night with loaded guns, watching over their loved ones.

Commissioner Wright had to issue an order for people to stay away from the police station and to stop following patrol cars when they went out to answer calls.

The authorities seemed to be everywhere. There were police officers, state patrolmen, and even two FBI agents on duty. They had come to Mattoon to try and figure out what kind of gas was used in the attacks.

But no one was having much luck in catching the Gasser. Not only did he attack the three locations just mentioned on Saturday night, September 10, but he also made a trip outside of town and struck a farmhouse that belonged to Mr. and Mrs. Stewart Scott.

The Scotts had been in town, volunteering for an armed patrol that was canceled by the police, and arrived home to their farm on the edge of Mattoon late in the evening. They found the house filled with sweet-smelling gas when they walked inside. Choking and gasping, they stumbled outside and called the county sheriff's office, which was working in conjunction with the Mattoon Police Department in trying to catch the Gasser.

No one was having much luck.

The attack on the Stewart farmhouse seems to mark a turning point in the story of Mattoon's Mad Gasser. It was almost as if the idea of the gas attacks leaving the city of Mattoon and going out to the country pushed the scales of official acceptance in the wrong direction.

As Commissioner Wright stated, "There is no doubt that a gas maniac exists and has made a number of attacks. But many of the reported attacks are nothing more than hysteria. Fear of the gas man is entirely out of proportion to the menace of the relatively harmless gas he is spraying. The whole town is sick with hysteria, and last night it spread out into the country."

In order to check the "hysteria," he now ordered that any person who the Gasser had attacked had to be taken to the Mattoon Memorial Hospital to determine if they were actually victims of the prowler or "of their own hysterical imaginations."

Even newspaper accounts - which had maintained a breathless tone through the whole affair - began to take a more skeptical look at the incident, placing "Mad Gasser" in quotes and stating, "no more genuine attacks reported." Ignoring witness accounts and evidence left at the scenes, the police began to dismiss new reports and suggested to victims they were "imagining things."

It was really all they could do. The whole thing had just gone too far. The Gasser could not be caught, identified, or tracked down. If they ignored the problem, it would go away. Besides, how could it be real? If he was real, how could he avoid capture for so long?

Psychology experts were quoted in the newspapers suggesting the women of Mattoon had dreamed up the "Gasser" as a desperate cry for attention, as many of their husbands were overseas fighting in the war.

This theory ignored the fact that many victims and witnesses were men and that this so-called "fantasy" left behind evidence of his existence.

On the night of September 11, the police received several calls of new attacks. By now, Mattoon officers were being assisted by the state police and three officers from Urbana. Using new mobile two-way broadcasting equipment, which made it unnecessary to operate from headquarters, they were able to arrive at the homes from which calls were made "only a few seconds" after the report had been telephoned to the police station.

Perfunctory efforts were made to investigate the new calls, and all but one was dismissed as a false alarm. Officers admitted there was evidence of a break-in at a home on the northwest side where a screen door had been cut to allow access to the lock. There was no odor of gas, though, so it likely wasn't anything to worry about.

One woman even helped the officials make their point. She was taken to Memorial Hospital after being "overcome by overwrought nerves" caused by the Gasser. A physician who examined her pronounced her case as one of "extreme mental anguish." He gave her a sedative and sent her home.

As far as the cops were concerned, the story was over.

On September 12, Commissioner Wright, Chief Cole, and Captain Harry Curtis from the State Police issued their final statement on the Mattoon gas attacks.

They never happened.

The "Mad Gasser" was a myth. He didn't exist.

The gas that had overwhelmed people in Mattoon - causing illness and paralysis -- was tetrachloride gas, which was used in large quantities by the Atlas Diesel Engine Company in Mattoon. It could be carried throughout the town by the wind, and it could have left the stain found on the salt bag found at the Cordes' home. In fact, workers from the Atlas plant likely threw it away, and it ended up on their porch.

The Gasser himself was simply a figment of residents' imaginations. The State Police had checked and re-checked all 35 "victims" stories and were convinced the Gasser did not exist. The whole case, Commissioner Wright said, "was a mistake from beginning to end."

Not surprisingly, W.J. Webster, a spokesman for the Atlas Diesel Engine plant - which had been turned to making gun shells for the war effort -- was quick to deny the allegations that his company had caused the concern in town. There were no fumes that could cause those effects, and even if they did, why had they not been reported before now? And how exactly was this gas cutting the window screens on Mattoon homes before causing nausea and paralysis?

"That statement is ridiculous," said State's Attorney William Kidwell, who lived in Mattoon. "Why, 60 to 75 feet across the street from that war plant are houses where the residents aren't bothered by the fumes. The plant has been using a cleaning substance - carbon tetrachloride - on gun shells ever since the war began, and there were never any complaints before."

Kidwell did admit that some of the reports of attacks might have been the result of mass hysteria but was firm in his belief that "someone did throw or squirt gas into some of the homes."

Captain Curtis noted that in the first cases reported, there probably was a house prowler, and the scare, plus the war plant fumes created the imaginary anesthetist.

It turned out that more people in Mattoon agreed with State's Attorney Kidwell than with the police. They were angry with the officials who refused to believe the reports of the Gasser. There were at least 35 people who claimed to be attacked. All reported the same effects of nausea, burned throats and mouths, swelling, and partial paralysis. The gases named by the police didn't cause these effects.

Besides, the "official" explanation also failed to explain the identical descriptions of the Gasser that had been reported. It also neglected to explain how different witnesses managed to report seeing a man of the Gasser's description fleeing the scene of an attack, even when the witness had no idea that an attack had taken place.

"Hysteria must be blamed for such seemingly accurate statements of supposed victims," Chief Cole said.

But Mattoon - and this author - wasn't buying it.

The last Gasser attack - or some kind of attack - occurred on September 13. I have never known how seriously to take this report, but it's possible that it was the last time that the Gasser struck in Mattoon. If it was, it was possibly the strangest attack of them all.

It occurred at the home of Mrs. Bertha Bench and her son, Orville. As in the other cases, a black-clad figure sprayed gas into a bedroom window and overpowered with them the fumes, causing sickness and paralysis.

But here's the weird thing - they were convinced that the Gasser was a woman dressed in men's clothing.

In fact, the next morning, they found footprints that appeared to have been made by a woman's shoes in the dirt below the window. And while this report does not match any of the earlier attacks in Mattoon, you might recall the claims of a woman's shoe prints from several attacks in Botetourt County in 1933 and 1934.

After that, the "Mad Gasser of Mattoon" was never seen or heard from again.

What is the truth behind what happened in Mattoon and Botetourt County? No one knows, and it's unlikely that we'll ever know. We do know that *something* took place in both places, no matter how weird it was, and theories abound about what actually occurred.

Was the Gasser real?

And if he was, who or what was he?

And if he was real, was he the same figure in both places?

It's hard to ignore the similarities between the two cases, from his method of operation to the unusual form of attacks. In Virginia, though, the Gasser was not always reported as being alone as he was in Mattoon, but then again, what about the identical reports of prints left by a woman's shoe?

Stories have suggested that Mattoon's Gasser was anything from a mad scientist to an ape-man --although who knows where that came from? -- and researchers today have their own theories, some of which are just as wild.

Could he have been some sort of extraterrestrial visitor using some sort of paralyzing agent to further a hidden agenda?

Could he have been some sort of odd inventor who was testing a new apparatus?

Interestingly, I received a letter in 2002 from a woman who explained to me that her father grew up in Mattoon during the time the gas attacks were taking place. He told her that there had been two sisters living in town at the time who had a brother who was allegedly insane. Several people in town believed that he was the Gasser, so his sisters locked him in the basement until they could have him committed to a mental institution. Her father told her that after he was sent away, the gas attacks stopped. Could this explain why the attacks stopped?

Or could the Gasser have been an agent of our own government, who came to an obscure Midwestern town to test some military gas that could be used in the war effort? It might be telling that once national attention came to Mattoon, the authorities began a policy of complete denial, and the attacks suddenly ceased. Coincidence?

Whoever, or whatever, he was, the "Mad Gasser" has vanished into time and, real or imagined, is only a memory in the world of the unknown.

Perhaps he was never here at all --- perhaps he was, as Donald M. Johnson wrote in the 1954 issue of the *Journal of Abnormal and Social Psychology*, simply a "shadowy manifestation of some unimaginable unknown." He was nothing more than a projection of the fears of wives who were left alone while their husbands went off to war.

But was he really?

I don't believe so. I have always believed that *something* happened in Mattoon - and Virginia - and agree with State's Attorney Kidwell that while some of the reports were likely the result of panic, there truly was someone spraying gas into windows in Mattoon.

How else do we explain the sightings of the "Mad Gasser" that were made by people who did not even know he existed?

Or identical sightings from independent witnesses who could not have possibly known that others had just spotted the same figure?

Those questions alone suggest to me that he was not the figment of "overworked imaginations" and comic books.

THE END

Who or what was the Mad Gasser?

And what about all the other sinister strangers that have ended up on the pages of this book - the Black Ghosts, the leaping attackers, the Killer Clowns, the Phantom Stabbers, and more?

Are they real? Imaginary? Logical explanations dressed up as something else? Or could they be, as some have suggested, visitors from dimensions outside our own, thus explaining their ability to appear and disappear at will? Are they figures so outside the realm of our imaginations that we will never be able to comprehend their motives or understand the reason why they did the seemingly unexplainable things they did?

Could the answer to the mystery really be as simple - and oh so complex - as a presence that can pass from one dimension to another, coming and going without explanation? Is that how they suddenly appear and then disappear and are never caught or captured, leaving their strange crimes unsolved?

I have no idea, but it's something to think about.

But maybe not something you want to think about later at night when you're all alone.

Because if this idea turns out to be true, where might the next sinister stranger appear?

BIBLIOGRAPHY

Bell, Karl -- *The Legend of Spring-heeled Jack*, Woodbridge, UK, Boydell Press, 2012

Citro, Joseph A. - *Passing Strange*, Shelburne, VT, Chapters Publishing, 1996

Clark, Jerome - Unexplained, Canton, MI, Visible Ink Press, 1999

Clark, Jerome and Loren Coleman - "The Mad Gasser of Mattoon" *FATE Magazine*, February 1972

Coleman, Loren - *Mysterious America*, New York, NY, Pocket, 2007 edition

Curran, Bob - *American Vampires*, Pompton Plains, NJ, New Page Books, 2013

D'Agostino, Thomas - *A History of Vampires in New England*, Charleston, SC, History Press, 2010

Dash, Mike -- 'Spring-heeled Jack To Victorian Bugaboo From Suburban Ghost,' *Fortean Studies 3*, 1996.

Dessem, Matthew - "The Wave of Evil Clown Sightings Is Nothing to Worry About. It Happens Every Few Years!" *Slate*, 2016

Fortean Times Magazine

Freeburg, Jessica and Natalie Fowler - *Monsters of the Midwest*, Cambridge, MN, Adventure Publications, 2016

Fulton, Wil - "The Twisted True Story of the Glowing Green Man, Charlie No-Face," *Thrillist*, 2017

Gerhard, Ken -- *Encounters with Flying Humanoids: Mothman, Manbirds, Gargoyles & Other Winged Beasts*, Woodbury, MN, Llewellyn, 2013

Godfrey, Linda - *I Know What I Saw*, New York, NY, Random House, 2019

Grey, Orrin - "The Bone-Chilling Legend of the Bunny Man Under the Bridge," *The Line-Up*, 2021

Keel, John - *Complete Guide to Mysterious Beings*, New York, NY, Doubleday, 1994

Lammle, Rob - "Mississippi's Phantom Barber of Pascagoula," *Mental Floss*, 2014

Matthews, Jack -- *The Mystery of Spring-Heeled Jack: From Victorian Legend to Steampunk Hero*, Rochester, VA, Destiny Books, 2016

Moran, Mark and Mark Sceurman - *Weird U.S.*, New York, NY, Barnes and Noble Publishing, 2004

Norman, Michael - *Haunted Homeland*, New York, NY, Forge Books, 2006

Okonowicz, Ed - *Monsters of Maryland*, Mechanicsburg, PA, Stackpole, 2012

Redfern, Nick - *The Monster Book*, Canton, MI, Visible Ink Press, 2017
------------------ - *The Slenderman Mysteries*, Newbury, MA, New Page Books, 2017

Romano, Aja - "The great clown panic of 2016 is a hoax. But the terrifying side of clowns is real," *Vox Media*, 2016

Scneck, Robert Damon - *Mrs. Wakeman and the Antichrist*, New York, NY, Penguin, 2014
-------------------------------- - *The President's Vampire*, San Antonio, TX, Anomalist Books, 2005

Shoemaker, Michael T - "The Mad Gasser of Botetourt," *FATE Magazine*, June 1985

Strange Magazine

Swancer, Brett - "The Creepy Mystery of the Phantom Clowns," *Mysterious Universe*, 2015

Taylor, Troy - *In the Boneyard*, Jacksonville, IL, American Hauntings Ink, 2020
------------------ - *Monsters of Illinois*, Mechanicsburg, PA, Stackpole, 2011
--------------- - *Mysterious Illinois*, Decatur, IL, Whitechapel Press, 2007
--------------- - *Without a Trace*, Chicago, IL, Whitechapel Press, 2010

Van Huss, William B. - *The Mad Gasser of Botetourt County*, Privately Printed, 2018

Vyner, J. "Mystery of Springheel Jack," *FATE Magazine*, October 1961

Alton Evening Telegraph - Alton, IL
Anaconda Standard - Anaconda, MT
Baltimore Sun
Belleville News-Democrat - Belleville, IL
Belvidere Daily Republican - Belvidere, IL
Bismarck Tribune - Bismarck, SD
Boston Globe
Bridgeport, Telegram - Bridgeport, CT
Brooklyn Daily Eagle - Brooklyn, NY
Butte Miner - Butte, MT
Chicago Chronicle
Chicago Tribune
Chillicothe Gazette - Chillicothe, OH
Decatur Daily Review - Decatur, IL
Decatur Herald - Decatur, IL
Decatur Herald-Dispatch - Decatur, IL
Dekalb Daily Chronicle - Dekalb, IL
Eau Claire Leader-Telegram - Eau Claire, WI
Harrisburg Telegraph - Harrisburg, PA
Hartford Courant - Hartford, CT
Kane Republican - Kane, PA
Kansas City Star
Kansas City Times
Lebanon Daily News - Lebanon, PA
Louisville Courier-Journal
Madison Capital Times - Madison, WI

Mattoon Journal-Gazette - Mattoon, IL
Meridien Daily Journal - Meridien, CT
New Philadelphia Daily Times - New Philadelphia, OH
New York Tribune
Oregon Daily Journal - Portland, OR
Paterson Morning Call - Paterson, NJ
Perth Amboy Evening News - Perth Amboy, NJ
Pittsburgh Post-Gazette
Pittsburgh Press
San Francisco Examiner
St. Joseph Gazette - St. Joseph, MO
St. Louis Post-Dispatch
Wisconsin State Journal - Madison, WI

SPECIAL THANKS TO:
April Slaughter: Cover Design and Artwork
Becky Ray: Editing and Proofreading
Lisa Taylor and Lux
Samantha Smith
Brianna Snow
Orrin and Rachel Taylor
Rene Kruse
Rachael Horath
Bethany Horath
Elyse and Thomas Reihner
John Winterbauer
Kaylan Schardan
Maggie and Packy Lundholm
Cody Beck
Tom and Michelle Bonadurer
Lydia Rhoades

Susan Kelly and Amy Bouyear
Cheryl Stamp and Sheryel Williams-Staab
Joelle Leitschuh and Tonya Leitschuh
And the entire crew of American Hauntings

ABOUT THE AUTHOR

Troy Taylor is the author of books on ghosts, hauntings, true crime, the unexplained, and the supernatural in America. He is also the founder of American Hauntings Ink, which offers books, ghost tours, events, and weekend excursions. He was born and raised in the Midwest and divides his time between Illinois and wherever the wind takes him.

See Troy's other titles at: **www.americanhauntingsink.com**

CPSIA information can be obtained
at www.ICGtesting.com
Printed in the USA
LVHW102059210222
711640LV00004B/213